LOVE, MIRACLES, AND ANIMAL HEALING

*A Veterinarian's Journey from
Physical Medicine to
Spiritual Understanding*

ALLEN M. SCHOEN, DVM, MS

and

PAM PROCTOR

SIMON & SCHUSTER

New York   London   Toronto   Sydney   Tokyo   Singapore

SIMON & SCHUSTER
Rockefeller Center
1230 Avenue of the Americas
New York, NY 10020

SIMON & SCHUSTER and colophon are registered trademarks
of Simon & Schuster Inc.

Designed by Irving Perkins Associates, Inc.

Manufactured in the United States of America

1   3   5   7   9   10   8   6   4   2

Library of Congress Cataloging-in-Publication Data
Schoen, Allen M.
Love, miracles, and animal healing : a veterinarian's journey from physical
medicine to spiritual understanding / Allen M. Schoen and Pam Proctor.
p.   cm.
Includes bibliographical references and index.
1. Alternative veterinary medicine.   2. Veterinary acupuncture.
3. Schoen, Allen M.   4. Veterinarians—New Hampshire—Biography.
I. Proctor, Pam, date.   II. Title.
SF745.5.S34   1995
636.089'58—dc20   95-1389
CIP
ISBN 0-684-80207-4

To all my teachers, two-legged, four-legged, and winged!

Contents

PART IV TEACHINGS

PART I

INITIATION

CHAPTER ONE

Megan's Miracles

Hear our humble prayer, O God, for our friends the animals, especially for animals who are suffering; for any that are hunted or lost, or deserted or frightened or hungry; for all that must be put to death. We entreat for them all thy mercy and pity and for those who deal with them we ask a heart of compassion and gentle hands and kindly words. Make us, ourselves, to be true friends to animals and so to share the blessings of the merciful.

—ALBERT SCHWEITZER

My awakening as a veterinarian began the day I met her.

She had the worst case of heartworm disease I had ever seen. Peering through a microscope at a slide smeared with her blood, I was aghast to see that her red blood cells were being crowded out by dozens of immature worms—a sure sign that the disease was in an advanced stage.

That could mean only one thing. By now, thousands of insidious "microfilaria," as the baby worms are called, had already multiplied and moved into her heart tissue. There, left untreated, they had grown into adult worms up to a foot long. Little by little, they would continue to fill up her heart until she died of heart failure.

With my stethoscope, I listened to her heart and lungs and knew from the coarse sound of her breathing that she didn't have much time left. But I also knew that I couldn't just abandon her. Even though I held out little hope that she would pull through the long, dangerous treatment, something about her compelled me to try to do everything in my power to save her.

With a sigh, I looked into the tired, pleading eyes of the sick, homeless golden retriever and made a promise: "If you make it, I'll keep you."

I called her Megan, a name that conjured up images of greatness. The Irish had popularized the name as a diminutive of Margaret. And like the moon, which the Greeks called Margarita, or "great pearl," Megan was for me a precious gift that I sensed would illuminate my life.

A friend of mine had found Megan in the little Yankee town of Jaffrey, New Hampshire, not far from Peterborough, where I had my first job as a veterinarian. Day after day, the forlorn creature would wander lethargically outside my friend's office, looking for a handout and a shred of kindness. Every few steps, she would collapse to the ground in paroxysms of coughing, then struggle to get up, and, a few steps later, collapse again.

There were no identification tags. Not even a collar to suggest that once, long ago, someone had loved and cared for her. She was alone, sick, and helpless.

My friend knew where to bring her. Just the week before, I had announced my new personal dog policy: "Because I'm so busy, I don't want a dog unless it's a golden retriever, completely trained, well mannered, sweet, and loving."

That was Megan. I was hooked the minute my friend brought her late one night to my little white cabin in the woods. She had the dearest face I had ever seen. As I patted her head and scratched under her chin, she immediately nuzzled up close, as though we were long lost friends.

With a detached, veterinarian's eye, I did a quick appraisal of her condition. She appeared to be about four years old, and although her dark gold coat was dull and dry, I could tell she had once been a beauty. Now, she looked old and haggard. Her gums were pale, and her hacking cough signaled the severity of her condition. I suspected the mosquito-borne heartworm disease, which was rampant in that part of New Hampshire. Any dog that did not receive preventive treatments was almost certain to be stricken.

I spent a sleepless night, with Megan at the foot of my bed.

Then the next morning I took her to my office and confirmed the diagnosis with a blood test.

The treatment that I began immediately was almost worse than the disease. Twice a day for the next two days, I injected a derivative of arsenic intravenously into Megan's bloodstream through a catheter in her front leg. The poison would slowly work its way through her system to kill off the deadly worms that were clogging her heart.

Megan must have sensed that I was trying to help her. I could tell because never once did she flinch from the needle or recoil like other dogs. Instead, she dutifully held out her paw, and as I took it in my hand to insert the IV needle, she seemed to whimper a mournful acknowledgment of my efforts.

For the next month, Megan had to be kept as quiet as possible to make sure that the remains of the dead worms were slowly reabsorbed by her body. In this delicate process, which is similar to what happens when a lump of sugar is dissolved in a cup of tea, cellular enzymes break down the worms bit by bit into chemicals that pass into the bloodstream. There, they are carried off and excreted as waste. The danger was that during this time, any physical exertion could cause chunks of the worms to dislodge and form clots that could block her lungs as well as her kidneys or liver.

I tried everything I could to keep her from moving around. During the day, I took her to the office and put her in a cage at the animal hospital, a cavernous former barn filled with about thirty different cages for recovering patients. In between appointments, I would run over to Megan, give her a pat on the head and a few words of encouragement, then rush back to my work. At night, I walked her to my car and brought her home to the cabin, where she would curl up on a thick, fluffy blanket in front of the wood stove. Many nights after a long day of work, I was out in the snow chopping wood to keep the fire stoked so that she would be comfortable.

Megan never failed to show her gratitude. When I came in from the cold with an armload of wood, she lifted her head and beckoned me to her for a warm hug. When I visited her cage at the hospital, she let me know by the tender look in her eyes

that the sound of my voice and the touch of my hand were all
she needed to hang in there for a little while longer.

Despite her inner calm, I was often uneasy. Like the father
of a newborn baby, I awoke some nights in a panic, afraid that
she had died in her sleep. I would scramble to the foot of the
bed, where she was lying nearly inert, and put my head down
by her nose to test her breathing. Only when I felt her breath
on my face and saw her body move up and down in the quiet
rhythms of respiration could I plop my head back down on the
pillow to sleep.

Day by day, she improved. After about a month, she was
strong enough to take the next phase of treatment—a series of
pills that would destroy any worm larvae still in her system.
After another month had passed, I brought her into the office
for a second blood test. By this time, her cough had gone,
there was a brightness to her eyes, and her coat had the beginnings of a healthy sheen.

"Well, girl, are you ready?" I asked.

With that, Megan held out her paw for me to draw more
blood. I prepared a slide, and what I saw through the microscope was miraculous. There, floating around in her plasma,
were big, healthy red blood cells. There wasn't a trace of the
heartworm, not even a wisp of microfilaria to hint at the horror
she had faced. By all appearances, she was completely cured.

My broad smile reflected my inner excitement. As I leaned
over to hug her, I must have communicated the overwhelming
joy I felt because Megan let out a couple of boisterous barks,
wagged her tail, and slobbered my face with kisses.

From that moment on, she came alive. As her health returned, the sweetness and warmth that had drawn me to her
in the first place took on a new dimension. She seemed to
possess a special gift for reaching out to others, a limitless
capacity to love. It was as though she had a wellspring of
maternal tenderness that created an instantaneous bond between her and her companions, no matter what the species. In
her quiet, unassuming way, she became a life-giving force,
reaching out to the sick animals that crossed her path and
nursing them back to health.

My first glimpse of Megan's special talents as a healer came one night in January, when I brought home an injured lamb that had been viciously attacked by a pack of wild dogs. Such packs are not uncommon in wooded areas like those just outside Peterborough. Stray and abandoned dogs band together and, for survival, revert to the hunting and stalking behavior of their ancestral natures. This particular pack had surrounded the lamb and was going in for the kill when they were scared off by the farmer's gunshots.

The lamb, limp and lifeless, was carried into my office by the farmer early in the evening, just near closing time. Her tiny body was covered with tooth puncture wounds, and it was clear from the depth of the bites that she had barely escaped being torn to shreds by the frenzied pack.

As quickly as I could, I rigged up an IV tube in her neck and started administering electrolyte solution to the lamb to treat her for shock. After about a half hour, she looked up from the examining table and began to show signs of improvement. But she was still so weak I didn't think she would make it through the night. To give the tiny lamb the best chance to survive, I decided to bring her home and let her sleep in front of the wood stove as Megan had done. That way I could keep her warm and also check on her through the night.

But from the minute the lamb got home, I didn't have a chance to play nurse. Megan immediately took over, pouring out every ounce of her maternal concern on this injured creature. She padded over to the lamb and gently began to lick her, clean her, and nuzzle her. Her tongue was like a poultice, bathing the ugly wounds in a soothing balm. As she went about her ministrations, she seemed to be hardly a dog at all. Where the pack of wild dogs had attacked the lamb with intent to kill, Megan nursed her, intent only on restoring her to health.

Although the lamb was barely moving, she roused herself to respond to Megan's attentions with a wan little bleat. Megan paused for a moment to listen to the *baaaaa,* then kept licking all the more. And when she had finished, she nestled down right alongside the lamb and guarded her all through the night. There wasn't any question about where her duty lay. Without any prompting, she chose to forgo the pleasures of her customary spot at the foot of my bed so that she could sleep with her charge.

Early the next morning, I was roused by Megan, who tugged at my covers and led me toward the door. Thinking the worst, I jumped out of bed and ran into the living room. There, standing before me on sturdy legs, was the lamb. And right alongside, like a proud mother, was Megan. Her tail was wagging wildly, and her tongue was hanging out of her mouth in a doggy sort of grin.

The very next day, we were able to send the lamb home to her farm. I say "we" because there was never any doubt in my mind about why the lamb had recovered so quickly. As a scientist I knew, of course, that the IV treatment for shock I had given that very first night had helped stabilize the lamb physically and set the stage for recovery. But in medicine there is often an intangible factor, a mysterious "something" that makes one patient get better and another fade away.

For the lamb, that something was Megan. In the deep communion between this canine Florence Nightingale and her patient, I could see a healing power that went far beyond anything I had learned in veterinary school. With her simple outpouring of love, Megan had touched the very essence of the other creature to cause a physical transformation within. The special bond that now existed between them had apparently energized the lamb and enabled her to respond positively to those complex inner chemical and electrical forces that can further the healing process.

From that day on, I began to look at Megan as a co-worker on my journey of healing. Often, when I had to go to the animal hospital late at night for an emergency, I would take her with me and let her roam the wards to see her "patients." I would watch in amazement as she went from cage to cage, licking the animals and caressing them. It didn't matter whether the creature was a dog, a cat, or a ferret. Her approach was always the same: love them, lick them, and sometimes even lie down with them. If an animal was too sick to stand up and reciprocate, she would simply lie down in front of the cage for a while to give comfort.

When Megan was around, any natural antipathy that might have existed between species seemed to disappear. One time she even acted as a midwife for a cat who had been rushed to the hospital at 3:00 A.M. while she was in the midst of giving birth. The cat, a Maine coon, had delivered one kitten at home, but another was stuck in the birth canal and she was howling in pain.

I had no choice but to do a cesarean section. With the owner holding down the cat and Megan pacing anxiously at the door, I administered anesthesia and prepared her for surgery. It was a race against the clock. With a few swift incisions with the scalpel, I opened up the uterus and breathed a sigh of relief. Two little gray balls of wet fur were still alive. Sadly, their little brother, who was lodged in the birth canal, didn't make it.

Carefully, I plucked the kittens from the womb and handed them to the owner. She cradled the kittens in her arms and carried them into the recovery room, where she laid them in a box I had lined with a soft towel. But the kittens, seeming quite disturbed without their mother, cried and cried.

It was their loud cries that summoned Megan into action. She rushed to the kittens' box and without even a pause started licking the amniotic fluid from their bodies. Instinctively, she seemed to understand that the mother cat, in a stupor from the anesthesia, was in no condition to care for her offspring.

The owner grew more and more agitated. As she watched Megan lick the helpless kittens, I could almost read the woman's thoughts: Would the dog suddenly become playful and toss one across the room? Would she turn vicious and cruelly attack them as they lay weak and blind? But then, just as I was about to step in and pull Megan away from the kittens, the look of concern on the owner's face softened into a smile. "She's like a surrogate mother!" she said in wonder.

To some dogs, mothering newborn kittens would have been an unnatural act. But for Megan, it was the most natural behavior in the world. Even more remarkable was that she had an uncanny sense of her true place in the scheme of things. As soon as the coon cat was well enough to join her kittens and start nursing them, Megan willingly stepped aside. There was no jockeying for power with the mother, no attempt to control the litter as though it were her own. Instead, standing quietly by the box, watching the contented kittens as they nursed, she wagged her tail in approval.

The cat and her kittens spent the rest of the night at the hospital, while Megan and I headed home to catch a few hours of sleep. By the time we arrived back at the hospital the next morning, the Maine coon was up and about, and in good enough shape to go home with her offspring.

Skeptics might argue that Megan's nursing instincts came from her breeding as a golden retriever. Most goldens are sweet and gentle, and that's why I had wanted one. But watching Megan as she related to other animals, I could see that there was more going on than just breeding. She radiated a special aura of acceptance and patience that broke through to even the most unlovable of creatures—and left them like putty in her paws.

There couldn't have been anything more unapproachable than this particular ferret sick with liver disease. He was so emaciated and jaundiced from illness that he was hard to be near without wincing. Ferrets can make wonderful pets, but they are also prone to nipping and are notoriously smelly due to glandular secretions that help them mate and mark their territory. This one's owner had made the mistake of putting him in mothballs—as though he were a fur coat—in an attempt to get rid of the odor.

The problem was that mothballs are highly toxic, and in just a few days the fumes started destroying the ferret's liver. By the time he was brought to me, he looked like a skinny, furry banana. His belly was yellow, his gums were yellow and bleeding, and he had lost so much weight from not eating that he was only about an inch in diameter. His foot-long body was as listless as a limp rope, and the look in his dull, glazed eyes suggested that he had just about given up.

Megan took one look at him and whimpered a cry of pity. I

set to work administering subcutaneous fluids to flush the poison from his system, and after a few days, he began to respond to the treatment. It was then that Megan jumped in with *her* treatment.

Every day, she would lie on the floor with the ferret and playfully push him to and fro with her snout. There wasn't an ounce of meanness in her method. Even when he grabbed her nose in his tiny teeth, she didn't flinch or retaliate. She just waited patiently until he let go and then nuzzled him softly with her nose.

After a week, the ferret was completely well. I'll never know how much of his healing was due to Megan's tender touch— the physical and spiritual bonding between living beings that can set off a physiologic chain reaction of recovery. But over the weeks and months, as I watched Megan move silently among my patients, selflessly dispensing her love treatments, I found myself yearning to have more of what she had. Deep inside, I felt a stirring, a nascent awareness that through her I was witnessing something near miraculous at a level of medical care that I didn't understand.

These miracles were never more apparent than during the moments when Megan gave her very lifeblood to other dogs through transfusions. Once, at midday, a burly young man in blood-soaked camouflage gear burst into the office with his German short-haired pointer limp in his arms.

"I've shot my dog! I've shot my dog!" he shouted in anguish.

The receptionist hustled him and the dog into the emergency ward, and with Megan close at my heels, I rushed in after them. In seconds, I had the dog on an examining table and was checking his vital signs. His blood pressure had dropped precipitously, and his gums were chalky white instead of a healthy pink. I pressed my finger down and released it to check his capillary refill time. But the gums stayed white, an indication that his heart wasn't pumping enough blood to the capillaries.

"The dog's in shock," I told the man. "First we must get him stabilized."

With the dog nearly motionless on the table, I inserted an IV catheter into his front leg and began to administer intravenous fluids and cortisone to bring his body chemistry back into balance. Out of the corner of my eye, I could see Megan sitting attentively by the door, watching and waiting.

By now, I could feel my adrenaline beginning to surge. "We've got to operate on him right away!" I said to the surgical nurse. "Blood's oozing out of his abdomen!"

The owner just held his pet's head in his hands and sobbed. "Please save him," he pleaded. "I love this dog. He's my best buddy."

The man and his pointer had been out hunting birds when he heard a rustling in the bushes. Without stopping to check the source of the noise, he had taken aim with his shotgun and fired. The pellets ripped through the pointer's abdomen, piercing his intestines.

"I still can't believe I shot him," he said. "If he makes it, I'll never hunt again."

"We'll do everything we can," I assured him. Gently, I took his arm and ushered him into a waiting room. With a nod, I beckoned to Megan to come sit by his side. I knew the man would need all the support he could get.

The operation took more than an hour. The dog's intestine was so perforated that I had to remove a six-inch section and suture the two ends back together. All of this required painstaking precision, and every ounce of my skill and concentration was focused on making the dog whole again. At that moment, nothing else in the world seemed to matter.

As for the pointer, what he had going for him was his youth. He was only about three years old, and he seemed to have a strong heart and lungs and good stamina. But he had lost so much blood before the operation that I was afraid that no amount of fitness or surgical wizardry could pull him through.

His last hope was a transfusion. As I sutured the final layer of skin, an image flashed into my mind: Megan! She was the only dog in the hospital that wasn't sick. If their blood types were compatible, she could be the one to give him a chance at life.

I drew some blood from the pointer and did a quick blood compatibility test. It matched Megan's!

There was no time to lose. I sprinted into the waiting room, where Megan was sitting with her head resting on the hunter's lap. Gently, I took her head in my hands and looked deep into her limpid brown eyes. "Megan, I need you," I said softly. "Will you help me?"

In an instant, I had her answer. And with her assent, a wave of love swept over me with such intensity that my fingers tingled. Dutifully, Megan followed me into the operating room and lay down on the floor. I knelt down beside her and held out my hand.

That was when the next miracle occurred. Without any hesitation, Megan extended her paw to receive the catheter that would serve as a conduit for her blood. Why she didn't struggle wildly and pull back as other dogs do, I'll never know for sure. Perhaps seared into the deep recesses of her memory were impressions of another room such as this where she had lain on the brink of death. The catheter may have been a reminder that once not long ago an intravenous treatment had saved her own life.

With the pointer still on the operating table, I rigged up the transfusion tube that would send Megan's life-giving blood to our patient. Megan's blood was soon coursing through the surgical tubing and into the pointer's vein. And with every drop of blood, the pointer seemed visibly to gain in strength. His breathing became more regular, and his color started to return.

Megan's watchful eyes took in everything—the pointer, the nurse moving back and forth, and the blood-filled tube that was a path to life. Finally, after I had taken a couple of hundred cubic centimeters of blood, I unhooked the catheter and bandaged Megan's paw. To help her regain strength after her blood donation, I gave her some fluids and vitamins.

We stayed in the operating room together until the pointer's anesthesia wore off. The minute he opened his eyes and picked up his head from the table, Megan, ever the nurse, stood up and with her tail wagging joyfully started to lick his face.

The pointer stayed with us a week. Every day during his recovery, his owner would stop in for an hour or so to visit. But there was someone else who was even more attentive: Megan. In her own way, she made it clear that until her patient was completely well, she wasn't about to abandon him. She hovered in front of his cage like a guardian angel. When he dozed, she dozed; and when he woke up, she jumped to her feet and stuck her nose through the cage to make contact. She even tagged along on his twice-daily walks with an aide. The minute they stepped outside, the two never stopped sniffing and rubbing and jostling each other as they frolicked down the road.

Once the pointer went home, Megan seemed to put him out of her mind. She quickly resumed her normal duties, caring for other "patients" at the hospital, and hanging around me at home. But a week later, when the dog came back for a checkup, it was clear that she hadn't forgotten him at all. She bounded up to him in the waiting room—wagging not just her tail but her whole behind—in celebration of their reunion.

The tie that drew them together was even deeper than the blood they shared. It had started with Megan's loving concern from the minute the pointer was carried into the emergency room. It had continued with her vigil at the hunter's side during the operation, and it had been made tangible with the gift of herself through the transfusion. Ultimately, the bond had been sealed through her "bedside manner"—her overflow of love for the pointer during his recovery.

But it was Megan's healing spirit that transcended all of these things. Through the outpouring of herself, she was able to strike a chord within her patients that reverberated with restorative power. And little by little, that same spirit began to touch and renew my own spirits. I realized that there was a part of my nature that had been buried by the rigid rationalism instilled in me in veterinary school. There, animals weren't so much patients as "cases"—a case of hip displasia, or renal failure, or paralysis. In that rarefied, scientific world, the sheer love of animals, a love that had drawn me into veterinary medi-

cine in the first place, had been slowly stifled and almost completely extinguished.

But through Megan's example, I found myself responding in
a new way to the animals I treated. And as I allowed myself to
give in to my feelings, I was becoming increasingly excited
about my work and about the vast potential for healing that
was before me. She had reawakened in me the kind of kinship
with animals that I had known instinctively as a child. Watching her nurse other animals, I began to understand that the
elemental bonds of nature were more powerful than anything
the scientific establishment had to offer. In those bonds were
the strands of love, of kindness, of physical and spiritual healing—the strands of life itself.

CHAPTER TWO

Answered Prayers

*If we open our eyes, if we open our minds, if we open
our hearts, we will find that this world is a magical
place.*

—CHÖGYAM TRUNGPA

For as long as I can remember, I wanted to be a veterinarian.
My grandfather claimed that the first words out of my mouth
were "I'm going to be an animal doctor."

It wasn't something I learned. I just knew, from the age of
two—years before I had any pets—that animals would be my
life. As soon as I could read, I filled my library with animal
books: *Black Beauty, Lassie Come Home, Born Free, My Life
with Animals.* When I was old enough to venture around my
neighborhood in Queens, New York, I rescued every injured
bird that had fallen out of a nest or every little spring peeper
that hopped onto the sidewalk, unaware of the dangers of being
trampled underfoot. All my neighbors knew that if they found
a sick animal of any sort, they could bring it to me and I would
try to nurse it back to health.

As a city kid, I had a rather limited view of the animal kingdom: frogs, sparrows, squirrels, and pigeons. Still, anything
that crawled, walked, or flew took on an almost mystical aura
for me. Each animal I encountered was a special gift, a won-
drous creation, pulsating with the mysterious energy of life. I
wanted to watch them, touch them, know them, and, wherever
possible, discover from them the sense of purpose that seemed
to radiate from their every movement.

When I was in third grade, I announced to my mother that

my future would be out in the countryside somewhere, helping animals that other people couldn't help. To my family it may have seemed like an unrealistic child's dream: an unlikely leap from the sidewalks of New York to a bucolic life caring for cows, horses, and sheep that might otherwise have been given up for lost. But to me, the dream was intensely real, and I played it over and over again in my mind.

Across from my house there was a bike path that led along a stretch of parkland that had somehow been saved from development. When I wanted to escape the city, I hopped on my bike and headed to the end of the path where on top of a knoll there was an apple tree that seemed specially made for sitting and dreaming. When no one was around, I would scramble up to the top of the tree, perch among the leaves, and stare at the big white puffy cumulus clouds drifting by overhead. For hours, I would imagine myself sitting atop the clouds and being transported to some heavenly, lush green place populated by animals of every kind. By any definition, it was a spiritual experience. And when my mother urged me to pay attention to more traditional religious observances, I would say, "I feel closer to God when I'm with nature."

As I grew older, my escapes grew more and more frequent. I hated high school. We lived in a tough neighborhood, and I preferred having as little to do with the kids my age as possible. So I spent much of my time painting—animals, of course—or fishing at a lake in Alley Pond Park, an oasis of woods, ponds, and marshland right in the middle of Queens. I never kept the fish I caught. If they were big, I let them go. But sometimes, if they were very small, I took them home, put them in a fish tank, and watched them for a while before returning them to their pond. For me, concentrating on the silent movements of the fish was an almost meditative experience. My mind would become empty and quiet, and as I gave myself over to their gentle pace, I would find myself totally at peace.

When I wasn't with my animal friends, I was restless. I felt a yearning to go beyond what I knew—to thrust myself into an environment where my mind could be stretched by new ideas and experiences. I got my chance the summer between my junior and senior years of high school when I was awarded a National Science Foundation grant to study biology for eight weeks at the University of Bridgeport. There, in the midst of dissections and discussions on the meaning of life, I found out where I belonged. This was the world I had been looking for, and by the end of the summer, I was ready to quit high school right then and there. Then, without my even asking, an insightful professor gave me my ticket to freedom: a full four-year scholarship to college at Bridgeport—beginning the very next week!

I dropped out of high school, entered college, and began an adventure in science and healing that continues to unfold. It didn't take long before I discovered that if I wanted to use science to serve the animals I cared about so deeply, I would have to make some difficult personal and ethical choices.

My first taste of the inner conflicts ahead came one summer during a coveted internship to study animal behavior at the American Museum of Natural History in New York. I was assigned to a research team studying the sexual behavior of cats. The scientists were interested in finding out whether cats produced scents that stimulated sexual arousal.

The problem was that to conduct the study the researchers had to remove surgically each cat's olfactory bulb—the part of the brain that governs the sense of smell. When I first heard about the procedure, I was shocked and even felt a little sick. Why maim a perfectly healthy animal? I wondered. But I kept my thoughts to myself because I was new at this research business and wasn't really sure what my personal position should be.

To observe the cats' sexual responses after they recovered from surgery, I would put a male and female into a room and record their interactions. On a purely scientific level, the assignment was a good introduction to research protocols. As it turned out, the removal of the olfactory bulb did play a role in the cats' sexual interactions. Instead of extended foreplay, such as nuzzling and sniffing, the cats went immediately into the sexual act.

But I still worried about the welfare of the cats. According to the scientists supervising the project, the surgery would have no effect on their longevity. I was told that all procedures had been done humanely and that every attempt had been made to minimize the cats' discomfort. Also, great pains would be taken to find them homes after the study was completed.

Still, such reassurances really didn't satisfy me. The idea of removing the olfactory bulb from a perfectly healthy cat—just to see if it responded sexually or not—remained repugnant. I didn't understand my feelings well enough to put them into words. I just knew I was in turmoil. I sensed that the surgery was violating the sanctity of nature, an unwritten law of the universe that gave a creature the right to live as God meant it to live—with its olfactory bulb intact!

My feelings about the cats were influenced by independent studies I was pursuing on Native Americans. Every week, I would pick up a new book on the subject from the museum bookstore, and as I rode the subway back and forth from the research project each day, I learned more and more about Native American cultures and philosophies. Their respect for life jumped out at me, and my reservations about the animal research deepened.

But I was just a student with little standing to object. So in the end, I kept my own counsel and did what I could to make the lives of the cats better. Every day, before the surgery, I went to work an hour early and played with them. After the operations, I came into the room where they were kept and gave them some water, stroked them, and talked to them. I put all my energy into giving them love. It wasn't simply a hobby I carved out for myself—it was a passionate calling.

But it remained to be seen exactly how my personal sense of a mission to help animals would fit into my future life. My career plans were at a crossroads during my last year at college. I was drawn to the traditional, "safe" path of medical school—a choice that I knew would please my parents. I had also worked one summer as a paramedical assistant with the Christian Medical Society in the Dominican Republic and Haiti, and felt a tug toward working with the sick in such impoverished areas. But my heart was leading me to become a veterinarian. I applied to school in both fields, and automatically assumed that getting into vet school would be considerably easier than making it into medical school. But in a strange turn of events, I was put on the waiting list at vet school—and was offered a scholarship to medical school.

Now I was more than a little confused about the path I should take. Should I seize the bird in the hand—medicine—and pursue a career working with people? Or should I take a risk, try again, and follow my original longing to become a veterinarian?

To find an answer, I did what I had always done as a child: when in doubt, I went back to nature. I jumped in the beat-up old Chevy I had been given for graduation and headed West. I had so little money that I didn't even have a tent. All I had was a sleeping bag and an old backpack with a knife, a flashlight, some fishing line, and a hook. I went from the Rockies to the Sierra Nevada to the Cascades, hiking alone along rugged trails that ended in desolate peaks where I would camp out under the stars. As I trekked along, playing hide-and-seek with marmots and black swallowtails and moose, I asked God to show me which path to take.

Then one day, out of nowhere, I seemed to hear a voice say, "I want you to become a veterinarian."

I didn't think it odd that God should speak to me directly. After all, I had been speaking to Him ever since my youthful musings in the apple tree in Queens. If God's temple is nature, as the ancient Jewish mystics of the Kabala had said, then it was only fitting that His voice should echo in the midst of His creation.

If I needed any confirmation of this revelation, I got it—in a dramatically symbolic stroke—on top of Mount Olympus, the highest peak in the Olympic Mountains in Washington State. With very little food in my pack, I had foolishly headed up the mountain's main slope. I expected that the trek would take only two days, but as two days stretched into three, I was beginning to get worried.

I had no choice but to do what Native Americans had done and live off the land. Luckily, I had taken a course in biosurvival in college. So I threw myself on the mercy of nature and foraged for wild carrots, onions, and dandelions along the trail. With my fishing line and hook, I caught a couple of fish in a mountain lake, grilled them on a stick over the fire, and settled down for an uneasy night's sleep.

About 2 A.M., I was suddenly awakened by the sound of crashing in the bushes. I grabbed my flashlight and tiptoed over to the source of the noise. As quietly as I could, I parted the bushes and beamed the flashlight into the blackness. There, just a few feet away, a struggle to the death was taking place between a ferret and a snake. The ferret held the snake tight between its teeth and was flipping it back and forth mercilessly. A few moments later, the snake grew limp. The ferret, no longer absorbed by the contest, turned his head toward the light and stared in my direction.

My body tingled with excitement. Here was nature in the raw —a primal environment in which I was just another inhabitant. In the wild, I realized the ferret and I were not really so different. Each of us was living from minute to minute, using our skill and resourcefulness to survive. But even more, I had a sense that somehow the ferret and I were interconnected. Perhaps he had actually saved me from danger by killing the snake. I'll never know. All I know is that as I watched the ferret slink off into the night, dragging the snake along with him, I no longer felt alone.

A few days later on the shores of Glacier Lake in Montana, I found another unexpected companion. I had been fishing for about an hour with no luck when suddenly I felt a tug at my line. And just as I was about to reel in what I hoped was my evening meal, a playful otter popped out of the water. His little face seemed to be grinning at some secret joke—until I realized that the joke was on me.

He dove back into the water and a few seconds later emerged triumphantly with a fish in his mouth. Then as if to mock me, he waved the fish back and forth at me, and dove back under again.

"Hey," I called out. "That's *my* fish!"

Otters are notorious clowns, and this one was enticing me

into a game. For the next hour or so, we engaged in a "conversation," as I continued to wait for a catch and he playfully bobbed and circled nearby. The sun was beginning to drop behind the mountain when at long last I made my first catch of the day.

"I got one!" I shouted, holding it up for my friend to admire.

"Eeek! Eeek!" he barked in approval. Then, with our game at a draw, he cocked his head, dove into the water, and swam away.

It didn't take long for me to start missing him. Somehow, we had understood each other, this otter and I. In our brief time together, communicating through gestures and sounds, we had developed the beginnings of a friendship. I had been comforted by his presence and buoyed by his spirited high jinks; he had clearly relished my companionship—especially the chance to perform for an audience.

As I made my way back to civilization, I realized that my wilderness trek had been a prelude to the much larger journey that lay ahead of me. Through the ferret that had protected me and the otter that had played with me, I began to understand that, somehow, nature itself was placing a seal of approval on my decision to devote my life in the service of animals. By the time I arrived home, I was firmly committed to putting all my energies into becoming an animal doctor.

My mother was devastated. When I announced that I was passing up a scholarship to medical school to throw my lot in with the creeping and crawling things of the earth, she took to bed for a week! But after listening to my thoughts, she understood my deep love for animals and my need to follow my calling, and she soon got over it. Before long I found myself working toward a graduate degree at the University of Illinois in what I hoped would be a first step toward vet school. Right from the start, I made my priorities clear to my advisor.

"I will not do any research that hurts animals," I told him.

That's how I ended up petting pigs. According to my advisor, a lot of farmers believed that their pigs grew bigger than those in large-scale commercial operations because the piglets got more attention. But no one had documented this phenomenon

—and he thought the experiment might be appropriate for my research in animal behavior.

I set up a program to study ten litters of pigs from birth to the twenty-first day of life. Half the pigs in each litter would be petted for a few minutes each day, while the other half would be left alone. With ten to fifteen pigs per litter, that meant I would have to pet more than fifty pigs per day.

But to me, petting pigs wasn't a burden. I was overjoyed that by taking a piglet in my arms and stroking it and talking to it, I'd actually be contributing something to scientific knowledge. Every morning, I got up at 5:30 A.M., threw on my coveralls, and rushed to the huge indoor facility where the pigs were kept. For two hours, amidst the oinks and smells of the pigsties, I petted the piglets one by one, and then returned them to their litters.

During the twenty-one-day petting period, and for the three months after I stopped stroking them, I monitored each piglet's weight gain, mortality, and position in the dominance order. I had fully expected that the farmers' instincts would be borne out—that the piglets that had been given more attention would be plumper and healthier. But surprisingly, there was no difference in weight gain or mortality between the piglets that had been petted and those that had been left alone. The difference was in the dominance order. The piglets that had been petted —literally stroked with love—turned out to be more dominant than their littermates.

Here was *Charlotte's Web* come to life. It was as though someone had shouted "Some pig!" to the piglets that had been stroked, thereby filling their porcine little souls with a heady dose of self-esteem. And that pride had somehow been communicated to their littermates that had not been stroked and they now showed deferential behavior to their siblings. The only difference between the two sets of pigs was love.

I was elated. This was science as I hoped it would be: learning about animals in a context of caring. Clearly, veterinary medicine was where I belonged. And my determination to become a vet was rewarded not long afterward, when I was given a scholarship to Cornell University Veterinary School. I was sure that I was now on a track that would provide me with all the tools I would need to help the animals I loved so dearly.

I was wrong. Cornell was and is considered by many to be the citadel of veterinary medicine. And today, the vet school is pioneering approaches to teaching that will draw students closer to their animal patients, rather than separate them by a wall of objective scientific inquiry. But at the time I was a student, pure science was the name of the game, and science was inextricably bound to the business of animal husbandry. With farm animals, our focus was on healing for the sake of better pork, milk, or beef production. The primary goal, it seemed, was to get the animals well enough to be slaughtered.

By my second year, I began to wonder if I had chosen the wrong field. Day after day, as I pored over my medical books and crammed for my exams, I could feel myself growing increasingly out of touch with animals. The only way I could maintain an emotional link to the creatures I respected so much was to pray. Before every biology lab, I would quietly bow my head and say a prayer of thanksgiving for the sacrifice of the animal I was about to dissect. Only then, after I had expressed my gratitude, could my soul be at peace.

Despite my reservations, I decided to stick with vet school and finish what I had begun. At the very least, I would have the best scientific education possible. If this was what veterinary medicine was all about, I would learn everything there was to learn about surgery, diagnosis, pathology, and pharmacology. So for the time being, I checked my feelings at the door of the classroom and immersed myself in the science of becoming a veterinarian.

But it wouldn't take much—just a cow and a few gallons of beer—to help me begin to recapture a vision of the expansive possibilities of animal healing.

CHAPTER THREE

From a Dose of Beer to a Kick in the Butt

It is for us to make the effort. The result is always in God's hands.

—Mahatma Gandhi

Sally's problems began when one of her four stomachs became displaced. It filled with gas and floated up like a balloon on the left side of her body. The result was that she went "off feed." For days, she wouldn't eat or drink a thing. Such a syndrome can spell disaster for any cow—even a normally robust Holstein like Sally. The usual course of antacids and intravenous fluids didn't help, and finally, I knew we had to operate.

I was working as a veterinarian's assistant on a summer job between semesters at Cornell. For the first time, I was living the pastoral life I had always dreamed of, treating cows, horses, sheep, and goats in the vast stretches of dairy farmland on the banks of Lake Ontario. Here, at last, was my chance to tend the sick, heal disease, and give animals like Sally a new chance at life.

To a student like me, there was nothing more exhilarating than plunging into surgery and, with a few cuts of the scalpel, working the magic that would bring a patient back to health. My mentor, Dr. Court Howard, and I opened Sally up, pricked her bloated stomach with a needle to release the gas, and sutured it to the bottom of her abdomen. After finishing up the job with some neat little sutures, I felt confident she would improve in short order.

Normally after such an operation, a cow bounces back in a couple of days. But Sally did not come around, despite the latest medical therapies. Instead, she got weaker and weaker. And it was clear that if something wasn't done immediately, the farmer who owned her would have no choice but to "ship" her to slaughter.

"I'd hate to ship her," he confessed. "She's such a sweet cow."

I agreed. One look at Sally's sad, sunken brown eyes was all the motivation I needed to go for a long shot. "Let me give her some beer," I said to Court.

I had been reading about old folk remedies, and beer was supposed to get the "rumen culture" going again. According to the folk wisdom, beer aided digestion and whetted the appetite by stimulating the bacteria in the rumen, the cow's first stomach, where the cellulose walls of hay are broken down by bacterial action.

Court was skeptical. "Allen, the farmer doesn't want to spend any more money on this cow," he said. "Let it be."

But I couldn't give up. If I didn't intervene, Sally's future would be on a plate marked "Fido." To allow her to come to such an end—without doing everything in my power to save her—would be a betrayal of every relationship I had ever had with an animal. What about the otter I had played with? The pigs I had petted? The horses I had prayed for? They had given me life-giving energy. How could I not do as much for Sally?

Court had a small barn on his property, with a couple of stalls that served as bovine recovery wards. So I pressed him to let me keep Sally in his barn and try my alcoholic remedy.

"Okay," he said finally. "You can keep her for a week—and I won't charge the farmer for something like this."

I bought gallons of the cheapest beer I could find and started pouring the stuff into Sally's stomach through a tube I stuck into her mouth. Twice a day, I raced back from whatever case I was on to administer my "treatment"—two quarts of beer and enough intravenous fluid to keep her hydrated.

Despite all my efforts, after two days Sally was still lethargic and completely uninterested in food. Even when I held up some hay to her mouth and whispered encouragement, she would just give me an indifferent gaze and slowly turn her head away.

I was almost ready to give up. The whole idea was beginning to seem rather harebrained, especially since my beer treatment was taking valuable time away from my other patients. I began to think that before I became a laughingstock, maybe I had better call it quits and just let nature take its course.

But something was prodding me to forge ahead. Maybe it was the image of Sally's gaunt face that kept flashing through my mind. Maybe it was my spiritual sense that this one cow's life was just as precious as that of any other creature in God's kingdom. Or maybe it was the gut feeling I had that, however hopeless the situation appeared, there was always a chance Sally could pull through. If the beer had worked for other cows, it just might work for her. Who knew? With only a couple of pints more, Sally might turn around.

For a few more days, I diligently force-fed her the beer, waiting expectantly as the contents of one bottle, and then the next, foamed down her gullet. Still, there were no signs of improvement—not even a drool of saliva to suggest that she might be sneaking a few bites.

Finally, on the fifth day, I showed up at Sally's stall—and was greeted with a series of unexpected but very welcome smacks and slurps. She was contentedly chewing her cud, which meant that she had already taken in a stomachful of food and had regurgitated it for another chew.

My first impulse was to fling my arms around Sally in a big hug. But afraid of disrupting her ruminations, I contented myself by gently stroking her head.

"Thatta girl," I said softly.

By the next day, Sally was munching huge mouthfuls of hay, and it was clear now that she was well enough to go home. The farmer arrived around noon to take her away, and his eyes actually welled up when he saw the dramatic change in her— and the telltale stalks of hay in her mouth. He shook my hand so hard in gratitude that I thought my bones would be crushed. When he finished exclaiming over his revitalized cow, I offered him some of the leftover beer and we sat by the side of Sally's stall drinking a celebratory toast.

The whole experience left me with a brief glimmer of insight —an inkling into the potential for healing beyond the conventional medical approaches in my textbooks. Ultimately, what had healed Sally wasn't some wonder drug but a treatment as old as the hills: a few gallons of beer, and a heavy dose of determination and caring. The cow was alive because I wasn't willing to take the "logical" course of action and let the farmer "ship" her. Instead, I allowed myself to go with my heart, to follow the intuition that whispered, "She *can* be healed. Don't be afraid to take a chance!"

As I was beginning to learn, such risks are part of the fine art of successful veterinary medicine. There is a dimension to treatment that sometimes defies logic, looks foolish, and can confound the most learned practitioners. I realized that if I wanted to cure the creatures that were put in my path, I had to be open to inner leadings that would allow the ancient mysteries of healing to unfold.

But I have to admit that at the time, such thoughts were pushed far from my mind by the all-consuming effort of learning the rudiments of the veterinary profession. That summer, as I went back to the more mundane tasks of taking blood from cows' tails and nursing colicky horses, my exhilaration over Sally's recovery faded. By the time I returned to school for my final year, the unconventional insights from the experience were all but forgotten and I crammed my brain full of scientific case studies, lists of differential diagnoses, and drug side effects.

But then, following my graduation from veterinary school, I moved to Peterborough, New Hampshire, and there, in the shadows of Mount Monadnock, a certain openness of spirit seemed to creep back into me. Peterborough itself was a picture-postcard New England town of 5,000 with steepled churches and white clapboard Colonial houses set in a landscape of rolling hills. The town, the model for Thornton Wilder's Grover's Corners in *Our Town,* has been the muse for scores of writers and artists who have drawn inspiration from its pristine beauty and quiet lifestyle.

It was into this world of soaring imagination and old-fashioned sensibilities that I stepped in June of 1978. I had signed on as the fourth vet in a practice headed by Dr. Forrest Tenney. At the time I came under his tutelage, he was nearing seventy and had achieved almost legendary stature as an animal healer in this part of the country. Tenney's reputation reached such heights that during World War II, when the newly discovered penicillin was being rationed for use at the battlefront, he was one of the first vets allowed doses of the antibiotic, to save a prize bull. To cure his patients, he relied on a palette of remedies that included modern science, folk medicine, alternative techniques like the laying on of hands, and just plain common sense.

Once, the story goes, Doc Tenney showed up at a barn to treat a cow and was told that the animal had died a few minutes before. Without skipping a beat, he ran over to the prostrate cow to administer his own version of CPR. He threw his body on top of her as hard as he could and jolted the cow into taking a breath. With that, he gave her a shot of epinephrine, a drug used as a heart stimulant, to get her heart beating rhythmically, and the cow started to come around.

By the time I got to know him, Doc Tenney wasn't up to such physical feats, and as the youngest member of the practice, it fell to me to back him up in case he got a call he couldn't handle. Typically, he would ring me up and in an offhanded way invite me to tag along.

"Shawn," he would say, giving an Irish twist to my last name. "Shawn, I've got a cow calving in a field. I think I can do it on my own, but just in case, why don't you come along?"

Of course, I couldn't refuse. I quickly realized that what I witnessed on these rounds with Doc Tenney was more than just an experienced veterinarian at work. It was my good fortune to be working closely with a remarkable healer, whose very presence charmed and soothed human and animal alike.

Doc Tenney's physical size wasn't particularly striking; even though he was solidly built, he was only about five foot five. The compelling thing about him was his tender touch. There was a sweetness and generosity of spirit that seemed to cover everyone in a cozy blanket of kindness. He would arrive at a barn, give the owner a comforting pat on the shoulder, and immediately put him at ease.

"There, there," he would say soothingly. "Everything's going to be all right. I'm just going to give your horse a shot or two and she'll be fine."

Then he would quietly walk over to the forlorn animal, and without giving a thought to whether it might kick or bite, he would gently administer a shot.

The result was extraordinary. It was as though he had passed a magic wand over the creatures under his care. We used to joke that he didn't even need to give an injection. All he had to do was shake a bottle at an animal and it would recover.

Doc Tenney also had a storehouse of folk wisdom and treatments that amazed me. Tucked away behind glass on shelves in his office were dozens of dusty amber bottles filled with herbal remedies. And each little bottle held secrets I had never even heard about in veterinary school.

There was buchu grass, a diuretic derived from the leaves of the buchu plant, which had none of the side effects of the modern drugs I had been taught to prescribe.

There was uva ursi, a urinary antiseptic and diuretic used for a variety of ailments from bladder infections to hemorrhoids.

There was gingerroot, a remedy for nausea and indigestion, which had been in use by the Chinese centuries before the birth of Christ.

These proven ancient remedies had become an integral part of Doc Tenney's practice. I struggled with the conflict between what I was taught at Cornell and what old Doc Tenney had successfully been using for decades out in the field. We were taught in vet school that we should accept only what was scientifically proven with double-blind studies. Yet what I saw in front of me were time-tested remedies and techniques that helped animals heal despite the lack of laboratory documentation. I learned quickly that if my black bag of sophisticated treatments failed to work, I could always count on him to dig deep into the arcane insights of the past for a solution.

If there was ever a time I needed a full bag of such veterinary tricks—from the purely scientific to the utterly unorthodox—it was when a colleague dispatched me to a barn northwest of Peterborough to tend to some sick cows owned by a farmer alleged to be a former Hell's Angel.

"I must warn you," my colleague said ominously. "This guy threw the last three vets off his property. I'm the only one he allows on. But it's time you got used to these things."

With my heart beating wildly, I hopped in my Volkswagen and headed north on the winding back roads of New Hampshire. As I bumped along, I tried to put some professional distance between myself and the man I was about to meet. But the afternoon shadows seemed to take on gargantuan human form, giving shape to my mounting fears. I remembered the killing at Altamont, where a group of Hell's Angels got into a murderous melee at a Rolling Stones concert. I had read about the raucous biker parties on Manhattan's Lower East Side. And I had seen the burly thugs, bodies swathed in black leather and heads crowned by helmets, screeching on their Harleys through the New England countryside on a warm summer's day.

I could almost picture my impending fate, emblazoned in a headline in the *Peterborough Transcript:* "Vet Decked by Irate Biker." Through these and other mental projections, I managed to work myself into such a state that I was as tense as a banjo string by the time I reached the farm.

It wasn't a big spread, just an old backyard dairy farm with a neat little house and a couple of dozen cows out back. As I pulled into the driveway, I spotted this big, strapping guy stepping out from between the cows and coming toward me. He wasn't smiling.

He was huge, about six-four, with a long gray ponytail, sleeveless black T-shirt, and tattoos splattered all over his forearms and biceps. According to local scuttlebutt, he had breezed through town on his motorcycle one day long ago and fallen in love with a farmer's daughter. The farmer had struck

a deal: "You marry my daughter, you've got to milk my cows."
So he got off his bike and took to the land.

We stopped a few feet from each other, and the biker looked
me straight in the eye. "The doc sent *you* over here, huh?" he
said skeptically.

I mustered a weak grin. "Yes. What's the problem?"

"That cow over there," he said, motioning with a flick of his
head. "She's off feed. See what you can do."

I headed over to the sick cow, while the biker went back to
his milking. The cow looked awful. She was gaunt and hunched
over, and there was an intensity in her eyes that seemed to
betray a deep inner pain.

I pulled out my stethoscope and listened to her heart, lungs,
and gut. Her heart was beating faster than normal, and her
breathing was unusually rapid and shallow. When she exhaled,
I could hear a faint grunting sound. I checked her gums, which
were pale and dry. Then I pulled on a shoulder-length rubber
glove to give her a rectal exam. The manure was loose and
watery, approaching diarrhea.

From the initial workup, I suspected that she had ketosis, a
syndrome in which the cow's metabolism changes drastically,
ruining her appetite. A whiff of her breath and I was sure of it.
A healthy cow's breath usually smells of fermentation. This
one's was sweet, a sign of abnormal blood sugar levels.

Just to be sure of my diagnosis, I did a quick urinalysis,
stroking under her vulva with a piece of straw to cause her to
urinate. I tested the urine with a keto stick, a kind of litmus test
that instantly measures the amount of ketones, a by-product
of faulty fat metabolism. Sure enough, her ketone level was
abnormally high.

At this point, I was so engrossed in my patient that I had
pretty much forgotten all about the biker. Like Sherlock
Holmes, I was busy piecing together the evidence that would
give me a clue to the cause of the disease and steer me toward
the right treatment.

There was a chance—a good chance, from what I could tell
—that the cow had eaten a nail along with her hay, causing
her digestion to go awry. The nail might have lodged in her

second stomach, the reticulum, possibly piercing the wall and endangering her heart. That could explain her rapid heartbeat and breathing. It could also explain why, when I pushed under her sternum, she coughed and winced in pain.

Suddenly, I heard footsteps behind me, and I looked up to find the biker, whose name was Joe, looming over my shoulder.

"Joe," I said, boldly putting myself on a first-name basis. "The cow's all messed up. I think she's got 'hardware disease.' She must have swallowed a nail or something, and it's stopping her from eating."

I fully expected that such a simplistic explanation would provoke more skepticism. But somehow, I couldn't bring myself to spit out the scientific diagnosis, "traumatic reticuloperitonitis," in front of a guy with tattoos on his arms. That might lead to real trouble.

I had picked the right approach. Instead of threatening me, Joe immediately broke into a big grin that was so engaging I couldn't help but drop all my defenses.

"That's what I like to hear," he said, pounding me on the back. "The last three vets who came here to fix one of my cows gave me some highfalutin name for a disease—and the cow still died. If my cow's got a nail in her stomach, I want to know it. Go ahead and try to fix it."

So, I had Joe's blessing, but I wasn't so sure he would be ready for the next step. According to my medical books, to get rid of the nail, I had to shoot a magnet into the cow's stomach with a balling gun, a device for administering pills. The magnet would stay in her stomach permanently, attracting the nail and any other metal objects that had been swallowed inadvertently. But before I could give her the magnet, I had to do something even more bizarre. I took out a compass and held it under her abdomen to check for the presence of a magnetic field.

"Hey, Doc," Joe said, taking a step toward me, "whatcha doing?" I half expected some crack like didn't I even know the direction the cow was heading. I took a deep breath and as calmly as I could explained to Joe that if the cow already had a magnet inside her, a second magnet could cause more harm than good. The two magnets could catch a piece of her stomach between them and might cause irreparable damage to the organ.

By now, Joe was getting so fascinated by the whole procedure that he eagerly crouched down next to me to follow my efforts at metal detection. The compass didn't budge—in other words, it was unlikely that another magnet was inside. With that, I enlisted Joe's help in putting the balling gun in the cow's mouth and shot my own magnet into her stomach. Before I left, I administered intravenous fluids and medications to balance the ketosis and gave her an injection of antibiotics to help treat any infection from the puncture wound. I left Joe with other medications and instructions.

"Call me tomorrow," I said. "I'm sure she's going to be just fine."

Joe personally escorted me to my car, and as I got behind the wheel, I could feel my shoulders drop in relief. So far, I was ahead of the game. I hadn't been thrown off the farm, and it seemed that Joe and I might even become friends.

He phoned the next day with the news. "The cow's picking up. She's eating again," he said. There was a friendly camaraderie in his voice, an openness that I hadn't heard before. But it was a couple of weeks later, when he called with another request for help, that I sensed we had moved to a genuine level of trust.

"Say, do you think you could stop by and check on one of my other cows?" Joe asked. "My Jersey isn't putting any weight on her leg, and I'm worried."

But this time when I got in the Volkswagen to head for his farm, I felt no apprehension. I had made it past one hurdle with Joe, and I was sure the next one would be easier. With New England farmers, you get one chance, and that's it. If they like you and trust you, you're in. If not, that's your last visit to their farm.

The lame cow's name was Jersey Belle, and like other Jerseys, she had enormous soft brown eyes and a tranquil expression that made her resemble a giant deer. But as I approached, the look in her eyes turned to fear. I understood why the minute I started to gently palpate her joints and lower back. At the very first touch, I could feel her body tighten up.

"Joe, I think she's got a displaced hip," I said. From what I could determine, the ligaments holding her hip joint in place had been torn, causing the ball of the femur to slip out of the socket. The result was that whenever she tried to walk on her right rear leg, she was barely able to touch it to the ground and cringed in pain.

Joe and I both knew the prognosis. Under normal circumstances, there was little alternative but to "ship" her. "Isn't there anything you can do?" he said imploringly. There was such an urgency in his voice that I knew I couldn't turn my back on the cow—or Joe—although I was in a quandary about what to do next.

Joe must have sensed my hesitation, because in the next few moments, this big bear of a man began spilling out his heart. "Look," he said. "This cow was born six years ago on the same day as my daughter. The girl loves this cow. I just can't send her away. You've *got* to help."

I scanned my memory banks for something—anything—that might work. But my years of scientific training came up short. Textbook knowledge had helped me cure one of his cows of hardware disease and diagnose Jersey Belle's ailment, but it couldn't give me the answer Joe was searching for.

He wanted nothing short of a miracle.

My only hope was Doc Tenney. I picked up the phone and told him the problem. Within seconds, he had a time-tested folk remedy that was no further away than my medical bag.

"Take some diluted iodine and inject it into three points on the hip," Doc Tenney said. He described to me how the three points form a triangle around the hip joint. "I don't know why it works," he admitted. "It just works!"

Years later, when I was studying acupuncture, I discovered that the three points Doc Tenney had described are actually important acupuncture points. When the iodine is injected, it acts as a counterirritant, increasing circulation in the affected area. Scar tissue then builds up around the points, enabling the cow to walk.

But at the time, even though the how and why of the iodine remedy was a mystery, that didn't matter. I just latched onto Doc Tenney's instructions and followed them to the letter. Then, as Doc Tenney would have done, I gave Joe a comforting pat on the shoulder as I took my leave.

"She's going to be all right," I assured him, trying my best to project an air of confidence. Oddly enough, despite a tiny twinge of doubt, I felt surprisingly certain of the outcome. Somehow I *knew* that Jersey Belle was going to make it.

Within a few days, the cow was able to put her leg down without wincing. After a week, she was putting her full weight on the leg and walking around the fields. A couple of years later, when I finally left Peterborough to start my own practice, Jersey Belle was still going strong.

The cow's recovery cemented my friendship with Joe and his family. There is something almost transcendent in the shared experience of healing, a force that acts as a kind of palliative to human relations. In his concern for Jersey Belle's recovery, Joe had discarded his rough, tough exterior shell and given me a glimpse of the sensitivity and tenderness underneath. As for me, my desire to respond to his plight had opened me to new possibilities of healing. I had been willing to go out on a limb with Doc Tenney's unconventional iodine treatment. Somehow, my unwitting "acupuncture" on Jersey Belle triggered not only a physical healing, but also the spiritual connection of friendship.

From then on, anytime I paid a visit to Joe's farm, his daughter would drop everything to give me an enthusiastic welcome. His wife would whip out a warm piece of apple pie and a steaming mug of coffee and would reiterate a standing invitation to come for dinner. Although I didn't impose on them often, I always knew that if I needed a break from the rigors of my workday, I could find comfortable conversation and down-to-earth homeyness in the companionship of a tough but soft-hearted farmer—who incidentally happened to be a former biker.

My experience with Jersey Belle set off a new burst of questions about the practice of my profession. My inquisitive and sometimes rebellious streak pushed me to look for answers when others said there were none. But with the iodine injections and the beer treatment, I had tangible evidence that a host of everyday miracles were not only available but were actually right under my nose! If something as simple as an injection of iodine or a drink of beer could prevent a cow from being "shipped," what else was possible? What was I overlooking? What other simple tools could I find to relieve suffering and give a surge of new life to animals that seemed to be facing a dead end?

From then on, I was on a perpetual adventure of discovery. Like a test pilot who pushes the edge of the "envelope" to set new records of speed and altitude, I tried to expand my reach and test the limits of my knowledge. It didn't take long before my relentless curiosity, and sometimes unorthodox treatment techniques, earned me the moniker "the professor."

Ironically, the case that may have done the most to establish my reputation in Peterborough wasn't particularly esoteric. A pregnant cow on a farm outside the town was having a difficult time delivering, and the farmer had called for help. When I arrived at the barn, I quickly lathered up my right arm with disinfectant and pulled on my shoulder-length rubber glove to do an internal exam. The cow was anchored in a stanchion, a yokelike device that prevented her from moving around. As the farmer held up the cow's tail, I tried to push my hand up her vagina to feel the position of the calf.

I could barely get my hand inside: something was blocking the birth canal. I removed my hand and gently probed inside her rectum to feel the position of the uterus.

It was severely twisted—about a 90-degree turn from its normal position. As it twisted, the uterus had effectively cut off the opening to the birth canal, preventing the calf from sliding out naturally.

"She's got a twisted uterus," I said to the farmer. "I'll have to do a C-section."

"Naw," he said matter-of-factly. "I don't want to pay for that. This isn't one of my best cows. I'll just ship her."

I couldn't help wincing at his bluntness. "Ship her": no matter how many times I had heard those words, I still couldn't get used to the finality of it all. And I couldn't understand how, with barely an afterthought, the farmer could relegate to death such a gentle animal that might still have a few good years left.

Dairy farming is a business. I knew that. When it comes to dollars and cents, some cows are simply worth more dead than alive. I also knew that some cows never did recover after a C-section, and that the price of calves was so low it was cheaper for the farmer to let the calf die than pay a few hundred dollars for the operation. But I had become a veterinarian because I loved animals. I wasn't there just for the farmer. I was also there for the cow. And if I wanted to keep this one and her calf alive, I had to think fast.

"You know," I said offhandedly, "there's an old technique I learned from some vets in New York that might save the cow and not cost you much. Why don't we give it a try?"

I could see the farmer's face perk up at the thought of getting his cow back for practically nothing. He nodded his head in approval.

"Do you have a wide plank?" I asked. "It sounds a little strange, but all we have to do is get her down on one side, put the plank on her belly, and while you're standing on the plank, we'll twist her body to the other side. Instead of untwisting the uterus, we'll untwist the cow!"

What I didn't tell the farmer was that I had never actually executed the whole procedure myself. The last time I had seen it done, *I* had been the one standing on the plank. And I had been so busy trying to keep my balance that the rest of the details were rather hazy.

"I don't know about this," said the farmer, looking a little suspicious. "The other vets never did anything like that."

But I convinced him that he had nothing to lose, and before long we were consumed by the job of getting the cow off her feet and down on her side. With the help of a few neighbors, we took the animal out of the stanchion, lassoed her head and feet, and like a bunch of cowboys, pulled her to the ground. She was lying on her right side with her legs pointing straight out in front of her.

Then I began the procedure. First, I made a ramp out of the

plank, placing it parallel to her outstretched legs and perpendicular to her body. One end of the plank lay on the cow's abdomen over the uterus; the other end was on the ground. Then I asked the farmer to literally "walk the plank," until he stood on top of the cow's abdomen. While his weight kept the uterus stationary, his friends and I tugged on the cow's legs and pulled them up and over in a 180-degree arc until she was lying on her opposite side with her legs now stretched out in the other direction. It was like moving the lever in a voting booth from one side to the other—only a lot heavier.

With the cow now lying on her left side, I put on my rubber glove to see if I could work my way up the birth canal. This time, I had no trouble reaching the calf. My hand slipped right up the vagina. The procedure had succeeded in untwisting her uterus. At the opening of the uterus, I could feel the calf's nose and two little feet, ready to burst forth. The calf was perfectly positioned for a normal birth. With the mother's cervix already dilated about eight inches, I knew she could deliver on her own.

The cow sensed that she was about to give birth, because she quickly lumbered to her feet. As if to herald the calf's arrival, she let out a melodious *moo.* Then she began straining to push out the baby. Within seconds, the calf popped out and landed on the ground with a thump. I quickly dipped my scalpel in iodine and then cut and tied the umbilical cord to set the newborn calf free.

Instantly, the mother began bathing her newborn, using her rough tongue to massage tiny muscles and lick the remains of the amniotic sac from the calf's body. This maternal act was the most natural thing in the world, a scene I had witnessed hundreds of times before. But at this time, in this place, the cow's instinctive response took on new meaning. For these two creatures that might have been put to death, the tender touch of a mother's tongue to her calf's body became an oblation—a gift of gratitude for the new life that had been given to them.

I stood in wonder at it all. A rough-hewn wooden plank. A newborn calf. And a farmer who now had two cows for the price of none.

Word travels fast around Peterborough, and the next morning one of my senior colleagues, Don Fritz, called me into his office.

"So, Professor," he said, "I hear you delivered a calf. You didn't have to do a C-section and ship her, eh? Not bad. Now tell me, what exactly *did* you do?"

From then on, whenever a problem case came up, Fritz sent "the professor" to the rescue. Sometimes, I could find the answers through careful diagnosis and modern medicine. At other times, the answers came through simple country remedies like Doc Tenney's iodine. And still other times, the answers didn't come from my efforts at all. They were given to me by some gracious unseen healing hand that left me humble and filled with amazement at mysteries I had yet to understand.

I realized just how much I had to learn the night Fritz dispatched me to "Hillbilly Mountain," a remote area outside of town that was inhabited by a group of self-reliant mountain people who lived simply and generally kept to themselves.

"Well, Professor," said Fritz, "I've got one that will challenge you. There's a horse up on Hillbilly Mountain. See what you can do."

"You're sending me up *there?*" I said incredulously. I had heard rumors about the place, and what I had heard didn't make me any too comfortable. Although I had never actually met any of the so-called hillbillies, I had sometimes seen them shopping in town with their beat-up pickup trucks and shotguns. They had fearsome reputations as rednecks who would as soon shoot you as say hello. Most people left them pretty much alone.

Fritz's parting words didn't do much to allay my fears. "Just keep in mind, they do everything on their own up there," he said. "They *never* call a vet."

It was pitch black as I drove up the hill where Fritz had directed me. When I got closer to my destination, I could see about a dozen vintage pickups that I figured had to date from the '40s or '50s. They were arranged in a circle, and their headlights were ablaze with light, illuminating the patch of ground in the center. A group of people were gathered by the trucks, and I shuddered at what might be ahead. From the looks of it, I might be stepping into the middle of some Klan ritual or arcane religious rite.

But as I got out of the car and walked closer to the circle, I could see an old chestnut mare curled up in a fetal position on the ground. Next to her, sobbing inconsolably, was a young woman who looked to be in her twenties. Her arms were encircling the mare's neck, and her head was buried in the horse's mane in a mournful embrace.

Out of the circle, a tall, thin man in worn overalls started coming toward me. He seemed to know who I was. "Hi, Doc," he said nonchalantly, giving me a strained smile. "I do the doctoring up here."

It was apparent that I was not necessarily welcome. I nodded my head agreeably and put on a friendly mask of inquisitiveness.

"I've tried everything on this horse," he continued, "but we can't get her up. We've yelled at her. We've pulled at her. We've given her whiskey. Nothing seems to work. We need you to put her to sleep."

"You need me to put her to sleep?" I repeated, trying to buy time while I figured out what to do. There was no way I was going to come in like some hired gun and just put a horse away. But I didn't want to offend the man, who was obviously the accepted animal expert in this community. Clearly, I had to break the news to him gently.

"Let's just have a look and see what's the matter," I suggested.

"She's too far gone for that," he said insistently. "I would have shot her myself, but that gal over there—she wouldn't hear of it." He gestured toward the young woman who was prostrate on top of the horse.

"It's her pony," he said. "She and the horse grew up together. It'll make it easier on all of us if you just tell her the horse has to go."

"I'm sure you've done everything possible," I said, "but I always like to see for myself."

I knelt down by the horse with a flashlight and checked the

gums. The color was good—a bright pink. Then I checked the heart with my stethoscope. The heartbeat was strong and steady. From what I could see from the physical exam, there wasn't a thing wrong with the horse except maybe age.

"I can't seem to find anything wrong," I said, puzzled.

The young woman looked at me wide-eyed, pleading anxiously for help. "Isn't there *anything* you can do?" she said.

I had no idea what to do next. I stood there for a few moments, stroking my beard and trying to collect my thoughts. Then a low murmur began to rise like a wave through the onlookers. They were obviously losing patience and interest. My time was running out.

"I really don't see anything wrong," I repeated, still trying to find an answer. Then, as if by reflex, I gave the horse a quick kick in the butt.

Suddenly, the animal shook her head back and forth, looked up, and got to her feet. It was as though a bolt of lightning had struck from the sky. First, there was a stunned silence. Then, the ragtag crowd—in their faded denim jackets, worn jeans, and weather-beaten John Deere caps—started to cheer.

"You've cured her! You've cured her!" they cried with delight. The young woman who owned the horse was literally jumping with joy and grinning from ear to ear.

I tried not to laugh. I was one lucky guy, and I knew it. But I kept the secret to myself.

"Now that she's standing, let me take another look," I said as authoritatively as I could. I did a quick checkup and gave the horse a shot of vitamins.

"Give me a call tomorrow and let me know how she's doing," I said, and as I turned to go, the young woman rushed over to me, threw her arms around me, and gave me a big hug.

"Thank you! Thank you!" she exclaimed.

I walked toward my car trailed like the Pied Piper by the Hillbilly Mountain crowd, including the self-styled vet.

"Thanks. See you again, Doc," he said. It was a promise, not a polite brush-off.

I drove down the mountain feeling light-headed, almost

giddy. "Thank you, God," I said aloud, shaking my head in disbelief.

Early the next morning, I was called out to a nearby barn and found the farmer abuzz with the news. "Hey, Doc, I hear you cured a pony up on the hill last night."

"How'd you hear that?" I asked.

"Everybody in town's talking about it," he said.

As proud as I was to be the talk of the town, deep inside I knew I couldn't take credit for curing the horse on Hillbilly Mountain. There was too much I didn't know to warrant my becoming cocky or complacent. I was a vehicle for healing—nothing more. I sensed that if I could keep that truth in the forefront of my mind, I might begin to discover an even broader array of healing gifts that still remained just beyond my reach.

PART II

BONDING

BONDING

CHAPTER FOUR

Listening

*Let a man decide upon his favorite animal and make
a study of it. Let him learn to understand its sounds
and motions. The animals want to communicate with
man. But Wakan-Tanka does not intend that they
should do so directly. Man must do the greater part
in securing an understanding.*

—BRAVE BUFFALO, STANDING ROCK RESERVATION

If we are honest with ourselves, all of us will admit to yearning
for a connection with animals. What we see in them is a living
reminder of what we have lost—a certain innocence of spirit,
freedom of action, and an ability to love unconditionally.

We want to be part of this world of theirs, to throb with the
rhythm of life that flows within them. Deep down we sense that
if we can only make a connection with another species, in
some powerful, mysterious way the bond will strengthen and
affirm us both.

But in order to begin to bond with animals, we have to step
outside ourselves and learn to communicate on their terms.
We have to hear, to touch, and to feel as they do—to abandon
ourselves totally to the inner workings of another creature's
heart.

It may seem like an impossible dream. After all, most of us
have spent a lifetime learning how to keep a distance from
others—even from our families—in order to accomplish our
goals. In the daily struggle to survive, we have built up walls of
protectiveness around our emotions and channeled our energies into accumulating tangible signs of success.

But we sense that this isn't how we were meant to be. The

animals whisper of another way, and we know they have something important to tell us. To hear what they have to say, the
first step is to learn how to listen.

Perhaps the person who has taught me the most about what
it means to listen to animals is my neighbor Penny Russianoff.
As a clinical psychologist and the daughter of two renowned
biologists, Penny has more than a passing knowledge about
communication of all kinds. But it was her own remarkable
experience with a sea lion in Australia that gave me insight
into the very concrete, practical ways we can open ourselves
up to animals—and discover how to truly listen.

LISTENING TO THE LANGUAGE OF LOVE

DANGER! DON'T GO NEAR THE ANIMALS!

The crude sign should have served as a warning. But Penny
Russianoff ignored the message and purposefully stepped onto
the beach, nestled in a hidden corner of Australia's Kangaroo
Island.

There, stretched out in the cove in front of her, were hundreds of sea lions, blanketing the shore as far as her eye could
see. Mesmerized by the sight, Penny sat down a good distance
away to simply enjoy them in their habitat. For the next few
minutes, she watched with delight as they cavorted around,
nursed their babies, and splashed back and forth in the water
catching fish.

Suddenly, the atmosphere changed. A huge grandfatherly
sea lion that appeared to weigh nearly a ton started moving in
her direction. Penny sat very still, hearing only the *flop, flop* of
his flippers on the sand as he drew within a few yards. Clearly,
the situation was now tinged with potential danger. There was
a brief window of opportunity for Penny to escape. But she
didn't move.

As the animal continued to approach, she did what had come
naturally to her in her many previous encounters with the
animal kingdom. She adopted a calm, nonthreatening position,

lying on her back with her throat fully exposed and her arms casually at her side. If the sea lion was like most mammals, she reasoned, her body language would send an immediate message: "Don't bother to fight because you've won already."

Penny felt no fear—not even a trace of trepidation at the prospect of a close encounter with a wild creature that was three times the size of the Incredible Hulk. In her more than three-quarters of a century on earth, she had always approached animals as her equals. This time was no different. All she wanted was to make a connection with the sea lion. With her mind free of judgment, her only thoughts were about keeping communication open.

"I hope I don't sneeze," she thought, knowing that even the slightest unexpected movement could be misinterpreted.

Flop, flop. By now the sea lion had drawn right up next to her and began licking her elbow. Still, she didn't move a muscle.

"I hope I don't burp!" she thought.

Apparently, there was something about her pliant, inviting posture that beckoned the sea lion to take even more liberties. He moved toward her head, brushed aside her hair, and licked her neck.

A thrill of excitement went through her. His tongue was smooth and strong against her skin, and she could feel his hot breath blasting against her neck. She knew she was walking a very narrow, dangerous line. But instead of recoiling from the contact, she felt herself relax even more as the sea lion moved slowly around to the other side of her body.

By now, all action on the beach had stopped. All the other sea lions, it seemed, had eyes fixed on their fellow creature, waiting to see what he would do next. Would he grab this strange being in his jaws? Swat her with a flipper? Toss her about like a circus ball?

Yet Penny felt strangely secure. She knew that at any moment she could be crushed by the gargantuan animal, but from what had passed between them so far, she expected nothing but gentleness. The tender touch of his tongue had told her she was in the presence of an affectionate friend.

The sea lion moved down her body to her left elbow, which he nuzzled and licked once or twice. Then, in a final act of friendship—or courtship, perhaps—he lumbered toward her feet, where he lay down flat and began massaging her soles with his tongue. Penny couldn't resist sneaking a peek. She raised her head slightly, and was astonished to see his tongue —about the size of a loaf of bread—working its way across her feet and toes.

He seemed to know every muscle, every tender spot to soothe and pamper her. For about six or seven minutes, as he stroked her feet rhythmically, she lay back on the sand and allowed herself to be swept up in the moment. Her body felt light, almost buoyant, as the fullness of their connection began to penetrate her whole being. His touch was but the physical expression of something she knew to be much deeper—an openness to interspecies communication that might best be described as a "language of love."

When the old sea lion was finished, he pulled himself up on his front flippers and walked about nine feet away. He stood in a proud, possessive stance, as if to announce to the crowd of assembled sea lions, "This is *my* territory. Don't come near here!"

With that, the other sea lions, who had been standing still as statues, relaxed and went back to their games.

Penny, too, felt free to move about. She sat up and started talking to her new friend, telling him in a soft voice how much she enjoyed being with him. Inside, she couldn't believe her good fortune. She was actually having a conversation with a wild animal face to face, and she had the feeling her messages were being received.

Dare she go a step farther? Slowly, she stood up and took a step toward the sea lion. In an instant, he drew himself up even taller and shot her a look that stopped her short.

"No!" he seemed to be saying.

Penny understood. For a brief moment, the interspecies barrier had been lowered. Penny and the sea lion had both let down their guard and had been open to hearing the other's inner call. Each had responded with warmth, affection, and respect. But now, the barrier had been raised again. The sea lion was telling her in his own way that it was time to say goodbye.

Penny's eyes filled with tears at the peculiar yet wonderful miracle that had transpired between them. Keeping her eyes fixed on his, slowly she backed up the stairs that led from the beach. Toward the top of the steps, she turned around to get her footing. When she looked back over her shoulder, she could see her friend still gazing right at her. Somehow, she knew without any question that if she ever returned to Kangaroo Island, the sea lion would recognize her and remember their special encounter.

Penny's bond with the sea lion may seem incredible, but it is a sample of a kind of communication that really is possible between species. If I have learned anything in my journey of healing, it's that with time and sensitivity, we can bond with almost any animal. They *do* talk to us—and they are longing for our response. In subtle and not so subtle ways, they communicate to us their needs and desires, joys and sorrows—if only we have the ears to hear.

Penny knows how to listen. She hears not just with her ears, but with all her faculties and sensitivities. Whether she is with her cats at home in nearby Sherman, Connecticut, or in the Australian outback, her ears, her eyes, her mind, and her body language are attuned to one thing alone: listening with her total being to the interspecies language of love.

Penny has experienced what studies of human-to-human interactions have shown for years: that good communication lies not just in what is said aloud, but also in the unspoken messages we transmit through our body language. In fact, according to Dr. Arthur Robertson, author of *Language of Effective Listening*, and one of the nation's foremost experts in effective listening skills, body language accounts for the greater share of all communication.

Penny's encounter with the sea lion illustrates the first of four major requirements for successful interspecies listening that I have discovered in my more than fifteen years in practice. They are:

• Hearing with the whole body
• Having the courage to be vulnerable
• Developing target vision
• Being free of judgment

I have seen these ingredients of effective listening recur again and again in my dealings with a wide variety of animals. I'm not talking about a set of arcane practices that only a few initiates can master. Instead, I'm suggesting some simple approaches to listening to our animal friends that each one of us can employ to cut through the superficial boundaries between us and unlock the mysterious connection we share. Now, let's explore the kind of courage it takes to be truly vulnerable.

A FIERCE WOLF AND A FRENZIED STALLION
The Courage to Be Vulnerable

Whenever I've pondered what it means to have the courage to be vulnerable—one of the most important prerequisites for listening to animals—my mind inevitably drifts back to the stories of St. Francis of Assisi, who was perhaps the greatest animal communicator of all time. From his writings and those of his followers, we know that Francis "talked" to animals of all kinds. He had an almost mystical relationship with nature, which he revered and cherished as an expression of God's goodness.

In that long-ago time, St. Francis drew on the power of God to confront a fierce wolf that was terrorizing the Italian countryside near the town of Gubbio. The starving wolf had been on a wild rampage of killing, attacking any animal or human in his path.

Over the objections of the townspeople, Francis boldly went out to the wolf's lair. When the wolf charged him with his fangs bared, Francis, unafraid, made the sign of the cross in front of the ferocious animal. The wolf immediately relaxed his gait and "shut his cruel mouth," according to an account in *The Little Flowers of St. Francis.*

"Come to me, Brother Wolf," Francis said, and at the same time commanded the animal not to hurt him or anyone else.

As the story goes, the wolf, hearing the words of Francis, "bowed its head and lay down at the Saint's feet, as though it had become a lamb." Together, Francis and the wolf made a peace pact. If the wolf promised never to do violence against the townspeople again, Francis pledged that the people would forgive him and no longer try to harm him. The wolf reportedly assented to the pact by "moving its body and tail and ears and by nodding its head."

The bond between St. Francis and the wolf was so strong that the wolf never broke his promise. And the townspeople, touched by the sight of the wolf walking docilely at Francis's side, forgave their former enemy and loved and cared for him until he died.

This story may be apocryphal, but for me it suggests the depth of communication that really is possible when you have the courage to open yourself up completely to an animal. I had such an experience in Denmark a few years ago, when I was invited by a group of veterinarians to demonstrate acupuncture techniques on a dangerous stallion.

I say "invited," but, in truth, I suspected that the situation was a setup. I had given a series of lectures on acupuncture to a group of veterinarians at a school outside of Copenhagen, and although the veterinarians seemed receptive, I could tell there was still some skepticism. To put me to the test, one of the organizers of the lecture series took me out to a barn and brought in a stallion that was so frantic no one had been able to get close enough to do a thorough examination.

He was one of the angriest and most anxious horses I had ever seen. An enormous Danish warmblood, measuring about

17 hands, he had to be practically pulled into the barn by his petrified handler, who tried to keep his body close to the horse to avoid getting kicked or stomped on.

The stallion was snorting and rearing his head back from the lead rein with such force that his front legs barely touched the ground. His ears were back in a classic posture of assault, and steam literally poured out of his nostrils as his breath hit the cold air.

As I stood in the middle of the barn analyzing the situation, I could see out of the corner of my eye that all the other vets had wisely run for cover behind bales of hay. They were laughing nervously and smirking to one another as if to say, "Let's just see him try to get near this horse."

I knew I had a lot to prove, but I was more concerned about the condition of the unfortunate horse. Someone must have dealt him a very cruel blow for him to be so afraid. I had seen horses like this before. More often than not they were racehorses, the victims of their own breeding. Born to run, they were often mistreated by trainers whose only interest was in their performance. As a result, such horses came to associate people with pain, and they would often do everything they could to avoid human contact.

That seemed to be the kind of horse I was dealing with here. He had once won prizes in dressage, I was told. But since a trailer accident, whenever anyone had tried to get on his back he would buck and throw the rider off instantly.

"Should we tranquilize this horse?" asked one of the veterinarians.

"Give me a second," I replied.

If I wanted to find out what was bothering the stallion, I knew I had to proceed with caution. Courage was one thing; foolhardiness was quite another. The stallion had the power of 1000 to 1500 pounds behind him. One kick and I could be gone —that was one of the dangers of an equine practice. So above all, I had to keep my wits about me and be savvy about the potential danger I was confronting. I couldn't just naïvely walk up to the horse and start "talking." I had to consciously think about where to stand, how to move, and when to speak.

But balancing my caution was the confidence I had gained through years of experience with hundreds of horses. I understood their reactions. As most horse people know, horses can sense who is afraid of them and who isn't. I knew that if I approached this horse calmly, with confidence and love, the chances were good that I could break through his fear. That's how most horses would react. But not all. Some are so caught up in their hostility that they can't release it, even in the face of tenderness and love.

Would this stallion tolerate my presence? His answer came almost immediately.

Looking him straight in the eye, I simply held out my hand, with palm upturned, and waited. The stallion took a few steps toward me, sniffed my hand, and snorted. Instead of flinching, I kept my hand outstretched and focused all my energies on sending him a positive mental message. "I'm here to help you," I thought. "I'm not here to hurt you. Let me know in a nice way where you hurt."

Whenever I'm in a potentially dangerous situation like this, I always ask the animal to tell me about his pain "in a nice way" so he knows not to buck or kick. Then I visualize my hands going over his head and back with a gentle, healing touch.

The stallion inched closer until we were nose to nose. He sniffed me, and I sniffed him back. Slowly, ever so slowly, I started to breathe with him at his pace. When he inhaled, I exhaled; when he exhaled, I inhaled. Our breath became as one, and for the next few minutes we just stood there together, breathing back and forth rhythmically.

As we breathed, I could feel him begin to relax. Finally, he gave a deep sigh, and I sensed he was telling me it was okay to begin my examination. He looked me right in the eye, as if he understood that I was trying to help him, though perplexed that no human had communicated in that way with him before.

Gently, I ran my hands over the acupuncture meridians, checking for sensitivity at different points. Some points, especially along the back, were incredibly reactive, causing muscle twitches when I applied even the slightest bit of pressure. Such sensitivity suggested to me that he was suffering a back problem or that his pelvis might be out of alignment.

No wonder he hadn't wanted anyone to ride him. When he had bucked and thrown his riders, he was literally trying to tell people, "Get off my back." But no one had really listened.

He knew I was listening. Even when my palpation of the acupuncture points caused him to flinch, he didn't lash out at me. Instead, he allowed me to palpate his body a second time for a chiropractic exam.

As I worked over his body with my fingers, the veterinarians behind the bales of hay watched in quiet amazement. But when I announced, "Now I'm going to insert the needles," they broke into a fit of laughter. It was clear that they still didn't believe what was happening right before their eyes.

The stallion looked at me, and I said in a soft voice, "I'm going to insert some needles—but don't worry."

One by one, I inserted the needles, starting with a point right in front of the shoulder. The minute I inserted the needle, the muscles of his neck—which had been so tight that the muscle fibers rippled like ropes under his skin—relaxed, and his head dropped down a few inches. After I inserted a few more needles in his back, he relaxed even more. His eyelids started drooping, and before long, his eyes closed, his head dropped down to his chest, and still standing next to me, he fell into a deep, dazed state.

With the horse fully relaxed, I was able to step up on a bale of hay and do chiropractic adjustments on his sacroiliac and lumbosacral area to correct his pelvic alignment. It was all over in just a few minutes.

"I'm done," I announced to the vets.

This time, they understood.

"Bravo!" they shouted, as one by one they emerged from behind their protective covering.

When the horse finally awoke from his daze a few minutes later, he nuzzled my arm and brushed up against me. In his own way, he was thanking me for releasing his pain. Because I had demonstrated the courage to be vulnerable—to break through his outer shell of anger and hear the hurting horse crying within—this once scared, suffering stallion had been able to trust to my ministrations.

But it takes more than courage to listen to our animal friends. It also requires a certain degree of what I call target vision: a willingness to narrow our focus so that we are totally "in sync" with an animal's movements and messages—no matter what the species.

EVEN TURTLES TALK
Developing Target Vision

Growing up in a small house in New York City, I had formed some of my deepest childhood relationships with my pets. And some of these friends of mine weren't warm, fuzzy, or cuddly. Since my mother worked all day long, she wouldn't allow me to have dogs or cats—so I got turtles! From this unlikely source, cold-blooded reptiles, I got my first lessons in the special communication that's possible between species.

I didn't set out to listen to my turtles. It happened naturally, simply because I gave them my undivided attention. This is what I came to call "target vision." Without really understanding the importance of what I was doing, I made sure that when we were together, we were alone and free of distractions. There was no radio blaring, no boisterous friends to throw lettuce leaves at them, and no TV to draw my mind away from their tiny movements. Instead, day after day, I zeroed in on the minutiae of their lives, seeking only to discern their needs and pleasures. And they, in turn, responded.

At first, I had an aquarium with about five or six terrapins. They're the little guys with the red ears, which were popular before all the scares over salmonella. Hard as it may be to believe, turtles are surprisingly intelligent and can be very affectionate. Every day, I would come home from school, flick on the light, and burst into my basement room where they were waiting. Immediately, the aquarium would come alive. The turtles would look up from what they were doing and scramble all over each other to try to reach me.

To some, the turtles' responsiveness might smack of classic Pavlovian conditioning. Weren't they simply responding to a shining light that alerted them to feeding time?

Perhaps. But if you've ever made eye contact with a turtle, you know that conditioning alone can't quite explain the *feelings* that are transmitted in those moments between reptile and human. I somehow sensed that in their own primitive way, the turtles were telling me that beneath their hard shells, they were actually soft, sensitive beings. Like me, they seemed to crave love and affection. They didn't have to say it in words. They said it over and over through a certain look in their eyes when I came into the room, and through the physical response of their bodies to my touch. I would reach into the tank, take one out, and start petting him on the back of the head. With that, he would lift up his head and let me caress the smooth skin under his neck. There was something more in this interaction than a mere need to be fed.

My bond with the terrapins grew so strong that before long, I added bigger turtles to my brood: first a soft-shelled turtle, then a Mississippi painted turtle, and finally a snapping turtle. They were a motley crew, but they all got along. The only exception was the snapping turtle, who was so aggressive I finally had to let him go after he bit into the soft-shelled turtle.

As for the others, every afternoon I would take out the whole group and let them crawl around the room. I would lie down on the floor and watch for hours as they explored every nook and cranny of their environment. During those hours, nothing else was more important than what those turtles were doing. To me, totally absorbed as I was in their lives, their soundless movements and bright eyes were like a siren song, calling me to share in their energy and curiosity. I felt as though I had been transported to a world far removed from my Queens basement. It was a more peaceful place, where the rhythms of life were slow and gentle, and happiness lay in the unadorned pleasure of being together.

The turtles opened the door for me to begin to experience the rich communication that's possible between people and animals if we use target vision to become absorbed in their world. But it took a defiant hawk to teach me another critical requirement for approaching animals with a listening ear: being free of judgment.

MESSAGE FROM A HAWK
Being Free of Judgment

I knew it wasn't just an accident that brought me together with the hawk. He was a red-tail, a beautiful brownish bird of prey with a tuft of white feathers on his breast and a streak of red across his tail. At the time I met him, my career had taken me to New Paltz, New York, where I was working in a practice specializing in small animals and wildlife. The bird was brought into my office one morning by a passerby who had picked him up off the road. The man had watched in horror as the hawk flew into an electrical wire, then plunged to the ground.

Paralyzed from the neck down, the hawk couldn't lift a wing or even a claw. All the poor creature could do was move his head back and forth. I took the massive, eighteen-inch bird in my hands and looked him straight in the eye. He shot me a proud, piercing look that froze me in my place. With nothing but his cold, sharp eyes, he was trying to defend himself. Even though he was paralyzed and in my hands, he was telling me unequivocally, "Don't you touch me!"

Most human beings assume that a bird of prey is distant and dangerous—totally unapproachable. In this situation, I even found myself being judgmental. The hawk was so off-putting that I wondered if I could relate to this animal the same way I connected with dogs or cats.

Yet, without uttering a sound, he had spoken to me. He had demanded my respect, and I gave it to him instantly. I also gave him a name—Hawkeye—after the intrepid backwoodsman in James Fenimore Cooper's *The Last of the Mohicans.* The name summed up everything about my newest patient, a majestic hunter and king of his domain who claimed the right to live on *his* terms.

Right then and there, I committed myself to his recovery. I was his only link to life, and whether he wanted my help or not, I would give myself over to him until he regained his former glory.

I knew that for such an independent creature, rehabilitation could mean only one thing: to fly on his own, without a trace of disability. But it seemed like an impossible task. Helping to heal a pet was one thing. But a wild bird? A raptor that had once soared above the trees ready to swoop groundward for his day's kill? Could I ever hope to communicate with such a creature?

As I watched him eyeing me angrily from the examining table, I realized that if I had any chance of hearing his special voice, I would have to free myself of any preconceptions. I would have to use every ounce of my creativity and concern to penetrate through his paralysis and pride. I had to accept him as he was, listen for his cues, and proceed at his pace.

Over the next three months, for an hour or so a day, I devoted myself to bringing Hawkeye back to health. To feed him, I brought in "frozen dinners." Nearby, the Raptor Center at the State University at New Paltz had a ready store of frozen mice. I would defrost a mouse, cut it in pieces, and feed it to him bit by bit.

At first, whenever I approached Hawkeye's cage, he would fix a beady eye on me and give me his cold, hard stare, as though he was contemplating an attack. Despite his defiance, I went about my business purposefully, feeding him the mice and keeping up a cheerful monologue about how good they tasted and how much energy they were giving him.

His response was to gobble the food greedily—and then glare at me until I fed him some more. But day after day, as he came to understand that he was dependent on me for his food, he changed. Whenever I walked toward his cage, his defiance faded and a glow of acceptance seemed to shine from his eyes.

Along with the frozen dinners came his daily physical therapy. My technician and I took turns moving his wings, stretching his legs, and massaging his neck. My goal was to strengthen the muscles and increase circulation, just as he would do himself if he were able.

Through this constant physical attention over a period of weeks, such a bond grew between us that he would start screeching for me as soon as he heard the sound of my voice. As for me, when I heard him call, I quickened my pace toward the room with his cage. I would open the door, poke my head in, and with the joy of encountering a close friend, I would say gently, "Hello, Hawkeye, buddy. How're you doing?"

Only then did his screeching stop.

Slowly, ever so slowly, he started to come around. With each passing day, as I nursed him and fed him, the incredible possibilities of healing were unfolding right before my eyes. Against the odds, this independent, suspicious, wild creature that had been paralyzed and who would have been written off as a terminal case by the rest of the medical establishment began to improve.

After about three weeks of physical therapy, I decided Hawkeye might be ready to try to walk. So I put him on the floor and waited. Tentatively, he took a step forward—but then he collapsed. I held him up as he again struggled to place one talon on the ground, and then the other.

He was still so weak that I had to massage him right then and there, carefully pulling and stretching his legs and claws. Several months later, I learned that I was unknowingly utilizing a form of acupressure or shiatsu—which is the art of massaging specific areas of the body used in acupuncture. But at the time, I was simply going on instinct in trying to exercise his body as best I could. Then, after a good massage, we went back to the task at hand—learning to walk. I would hold him up, he would put one foot in front of the other, and together we would "stroll" along the floor.

His condition improved daily. As soon as he was able to walk on his own, I decided why not go for broke? It was time to start getting him ready to fly. We had a large meshed-in aviary outside, which was perfect for our trial takeoffs. Like some medieval lord, I put a leather gauntlet on my arm and attached long leather straps to the hawk.

Hawkeye clutched my arm with his talons and started flapping his wings. The flutter of those once-inert wings sent a thrill through me, and I remembered how as a ten-year-old I had raised a baby starling and taught him to fly. His claws would grip my finger, and as I raised my arm up and down, he flapped his wings until he was ready, at last, to take off.

Now, on a much more dramatic scale, I was doing a similar thing with Hawkeye. I moved my arm up and down, and, like the starling, the hawk flapped his wings harder and harder to keep from falling. He clung to my arm for a few days, then he bravely took off—and immediately headed straight down! I cringed in pain as he landed with a thud at my feet.

But Hawkeye didn't give up. He looked at me, and with eyes that were at once imploring and determined, he seemed to say, "I *must* keep going."

With that, I put him back on my arm and we tried again. He kept leaping and falling again until finally, a few days later, he managed to fly two feet before falling.

Then one day I released the straps and he flew up to one of the beams that were arranged like branches at the top of the aviary. He would hop along the beam and then fly to another one, slowly testing his newfound strength. Eventually, he was able to fly around the entire aviary. For hours he would fly back and forth, gripping the wire mesh on the sides, as though begging to be released outside.

Finally, when he seemed fully healed, I let him go outside the aviary. He took off from my arm and circled around and around overhead, as though clinging to invisible tethers. Perhaps it was his way of holding on as long as he could to his now familiar world of frozen mice and human friendship. For a week or two, he hung around outside, staying in the trees and screeching when he wanted his food.

Then, one day, he disappeared. Just like that. I stood searching the treetops, longing for some glimpse of him, but I knew he was gone forever. My emotions warred between pride and sorrow. I had poured out myself to help heal this hawk, and now he had abandoned me. I felt like a father who had sent his son on some far-off adventure that could not be shared.

But I wasn't left empty-handed. In his place, Hawkeye had given me a precious gift that propelled me on an incredible adventure of my own. By a stroke of fate, a charged electrical wire, I had been afforded the privilege of penetrating the inner world of a wild, rapacious creature, an animal that was born to kill.

From the beginning Hawkeye had set the pace. Instinctively he had thrown up a wall of hostility to protect himself from harm. But as I had patiently and humbly cared for him and listened attentively to the signals he gave me, he had dropped his guard and revealed to me his courage, his determination, and his capacity to care.

Hawkeye had given me a window on what may be nature's greatest secret: that no creature can remain forever closed to the healing power of love. I knew that if I could establish an intimate relationship with a bird of prey, I could communicate with *any* animal, no matter how distant or fearsome it might appear to be. All I would need was a sensitivity of spirit, a willingness to open myself nonjudgmentally to a dimension of reality where feathers, fur, skin, scales, or hair are stripped away—and where the only language is love.

Hawkeye had his freedom, and now I had mine. He had given me my wings, and I was ready to soar.

CHAPTER FIVE

Touching

Now when the sun was setting, all those who had any
that were sick with various diseases brought them to
him; and he laid his hands on every one of them and
healed them.

—LUKE 4:40

There's something about touching another living being that goes far beyond the mere pressing of flesh to flesh, or fur to fur. When a horse nuzzles another horse on a Texas spread or a cow licks a passing hiker in the Swiss Alps, all time seems to stop. For a few flickering moments, the two creatures are forged together in an inexplicable bond.

What is transmitted in those moments of physical contact no one knows for sure. But somehow the simple act of touching becomes a channel for transformation—a conduit through which the closeness, warmth, and energy of life seem to flow from one being to another.

One of my fondest memories from college was the change that took place in my little kitten, Blue, through the nurturing touch of a frisky puppy. When I first got him, Blue was only five weeks old and had been orphaned before he was weaned from his mother. I had picked him out from a boxful of kittens because I was charmed by his "outfit." He was black with little white paws that made him look as if he was dressed in a tuxedo and sneakers.

But as cute as he was, it was clear from the start that he was frightened and unhappy. Often, he would cower in a corner and emit plaintive little mews that were close to a cry. He was desperate to suck on something, *anything,* and he never seemed to be satisfied. Something was missing—and that something was a mother who could comfort and cuddle him.

When my roommates got a new puppy, a mutt they named Shaboo, Blue's life took on a new dimension. Immediately the two started playing together as though they were brothers. They would chase each other up and down the stairs and whizz around the house at dizzying speed. At mealtimes, they didn't hesitate to eat out of each other's bowl. As they cavorted together, they appeared to be one species: Blue seemed to think Shaboo was a big cat, and Shaboo acted as though Blue were a small dog.

I was certain that Blue's newfound happiness came from having a playmate. But I soon discovered that there was also something much deeper going on between this puppy and kitten. One day I came home from school and was startled by a sight that was both incongruous and endearing. There on the living room floor was Blue, nursing on Shaboo's tiny nipples! Like a mother, Shaboo was lying on his side in quiet repose, looking fondly at the kitten sucking away contentedly. It was an extraordinary scene that made me think of that ancient Roman statue of Romulus and Remus, suckling at the teats of the she-wolf that cared for them when they were abandoned.

Of course, Blue wasn't getting any milk, but that didn't seem to matter to either of them. What did matter was the physical link that had been forged between them—a link that continued to flourish over the eight months they were together. Even as they got older, every day they would cement their bond through the intimate act of touching. They would lie down together for five minutes or so, as big shaggy Shaboo "nursed" his little feline friend.

Through Shaboo's tender act of connecting with Blue, I began to understand that the power of touch is not only founded on the outward, tactile connection between two beings, but is also rooted deep in the psyche, in the forces of

- A touch that is caring
- A touch that is enduring
- A touch that is transcendent

My understanding of these forces deepened as I encountered other creatures that had been transformed by the power of touch.

A TALE OF TWO TABBIES
A Touch That Is Caring

The old gray tabby's pelvis was fractured so badly he couldn't stand. He had been sideswiped by a car, but luckily his fractures were such that they would heal naturally over time without an operation. Although he didn't appear to have any other injuries, it was critical that I keep him in the clinic for a few days just to be sure there was nothing else wrong.

"You don't understand," his owner said pleadingly. "This cat is seventeen and I have another one just like him at home. They were littermates, and they've never been apart a day in their lives. You've *got* to let me bring him home."

There was no way I could release the cat, no matter how emotionally wrenching the separation might be. Until he was able to stand and had bladder and bowel control, I had no choice but to keep him under observation.

"I'm sorry," I said. "It's best for the cat if he stays."

By the next morning, I wasn't so sure. The tabby gazed into space with such a vacant look in his eye that it seemed he had already given up and died. His vital signs were normal, but there was no life in him. He didn't meow. He didn't purr. He just lay there without eating, staring into some distant place where all hope was extinguished.

As I pondered what to do next, the phone rang. It was the tabby's owner, and he was frantic. "My other cat's been screaming nonstop," he complained. "He never went to sleep —just prowled around searching and meowing. You have to *do* something."

"I don't know if it will make a difference," I said, "but why don't you bring the other cat here?"

The owner made it to the clinic in twenty minutes. When he

walked in with the other cat under his arm, I thought I was seeing double. The brother cat was the image of his litter-mate—a fluffy pearl gray with stripes. But while his injured sibling lay in a cage torpid in depression, this one was taut with anxious energy.

The minute I opened the cage door, the healing began. The electricity between the two cats was palpable. At the sight of his brother, the ailing cat's eyes brightened, his ears perked up, and he struggled in a futile effort to get up and draw near to him.

But it was his brother's caring touch that really made the injured cat come alive. He bounded into the cage, rushed up to his brother, and meowing with joy, began licking and sniffing him all over. With the all-important physical link reestablished, the hurt cat mewed in response, and mustering all of his strength, reciprocated by licking any part of his brother's body that brushed by him. A leg, a tail, an ear, a shoulder—all were touched by his tongue.

The two cats couldn't seem to get enough of each other. They kept licking, and cleaning, and smelling, oblivious to any-thing but each other. They made it clear that for the rest of the clinic stay, they would be in the cage together.

That night, I peeked into the cage and saw that the cats were still inseparable. They were huddled close together, purring in unison, as the brother cat encircled his hurt twin with the loving warmth of his body.

After about three days, the hurt cat began to have normal bowel movements and had regained bladder control, which suggested that he had no further significant internal injuries. By the fourth day, he was able to stand on his own, with the help of his brother. The brother nudged him with his nose a few times, and the injured cat got the message. Haltingly, he struggled to his feet, leaning briefly against his brother for support. A few seconds later, he stood proudly on his own and took a few wobbly steps.

The next day, they went home. I didn't see them again until two years later, when they came in for a checkup. By then, they were nineteen and still in good health. The injured cat had fully recovered and never showed any ill effects of the accident. The healing had resulted not from some medical breakthrough or traditional veterinary science, but from the tender touch of a brother, whose physical acts of love helped bring about the recovery.

Observing interactions like the one involving the two tabbies, I have been impressed by how powerful and far-reaching caring physical contact can be. In particular, I'm reminded of research that has documented the importance of an attitude of caring in human healing through the laying on of hands. Dolores Krieger, a former New York University professor of nursing, conducted pioneering studies on the subject back in the early 1970s and discovered that patients who were treated by the laying on of hands had a higher hemoglobin count—the pigment in the bloodstream that carries life-giving oxygen to the cells—than those without such treatment.

Clearly, something positive is happening within the body when a patient is touched. However, this salutary physiological response doesn't necessarily correlate with healing. Searching for the curative secret in a simple touch, Krieger discovered that what counted most was whether or not the nurses *cared* about their patients. In some mysterious way, that caring attitude was transferred through the nurse's hands to the patient, and thereby stimulated a healing response.

That's what I seem to have witnessed with the two tabbies—a profound caring that had been transferred from one to the other through the touch of a tongue. And that physical contact had brought the gift of life.

But there is an additional dimension to touch that's also important—an enduring commitment to ongoing physical involvement. I'm not talking about an occasional pat on the head, but rather the daily, intimate ministrations that are absolutely essential to permanent bonding. A few years ago, when I was a young vet, I saw this close, ongoing kind of commitment unfold before my eyes in the profound devotion between a young man named Bill and his severely paralyzed dog.

A CURE FOR COONHOUND PARALYSIS
A Touch That Is Enduring

The dog was limp as a wet towel, with his tongue hanging out and a steady stream of saliva drooling from his mouth. He couldn't move a muscle below his neck. From his hollow, sorrowful eyes, I could see that he was overcome by exhaustion.

"What's going on?" his eyes seemed to say.

At first, I thought he might have broken his back. "Did he take a fall or get hit by a car?" I asked his owner, Bill, a young man about my age who managed a mountaineering store in New Hampshire.

Bill couldn't recall anything specific. All he knew was that the day before, Dash, a Labrador retriever crossbreed, had run off for a few hours. When he returned, his back legs were so weak they were beginning to drag behind him. Overnight, he had become almost completely paralyzed.

I pinched Dash's toes to see if he had any feeling at all. His feet and legs showed no response, but with every pinch, his eyes flinched a little and he uttered a low whine.

At least his spinal cord hadn't been severed, I thought. Messages from his hind legs were obviously getting through to his brain. His reflexes, too, were intact. A short tap on his knee with a hammer triggered an involuntary jerk, and when I pinched his tail, his eyes squinted in response.

After an x-ray revealed no broken bones, I found myself facing a puzzle. Maybe Dash had been kicked by a horse or had suffered some other trauma that had caused bleeding into the spinal cord. That could sometimes cause acute paralysis. There was also the possibility of a tumor, though cancer symptoms rarely appear all of a sudden.

Maybe he had been poisoned. Or he could have picked up some toxic bacteria in a pool of water and contracted meningitis. But Dash's preliminary blood tests were all normal. There were no strange bacteria floating around in his system—nothing to indicate an infection. What else could it be?

I went back to the examining table and slowly probed every

inch of Dash's body with my fingers. I was looking for something, anything, that would give me a clue as to why a perfectly
healthy seven-year-old dog had turned into a quadriplegic
without any warning.

Dash was panting softly as I probed behind his ears and
worked my way down his neck. As my fingers moved over
his skin, I suddenly came across something I had previously
overlooked—two little punctures the size of pinholes, about
an inch apart.

"Looks like puncture wounds, maybe a bite of some sort," I
said to Bill.

A parade of animals marched through my mind, and I tried
to picture one after the other snaring Dash's neck between its
teeth. Another dog? A weasel? A raccoon?

By now, my mind was racing. At the thought of raccoons, I
suddenly remembered an obscure disease my neurology professor had discussed and that I had read about in my medical
books. Coonhound paralysis. It *had* to be coonhound paralysis.

This disease is a rare ailment without any known cause,
which is usually found in hounds that are in frequent contact
with raccoons. The illness has a human counterpart, Guillain-
Barré syndrome, which has similarly devastating consequences. In dogs, the bite of a raccoon, or sometimes even a
rabies vaccination, can set off an immune reaction that causes
progressive paralysis. If the nerves of the diaphragm become
paralyzed, the dog can suffocate to death.

Dash was no coonhound, but it sure looked as though he
had the disease. If I were a gambler, I would have staked my
money on it. But just to be sure, I suggested that Bill take him
to a neurologist at Angell Memorial Animal Hospital in Boston.
We rigged up a stretcher out of a piece of plywood and some
old blankets, hoisted Dash on top, and put him in the back seat
of Bill's car for the hour-and-a-half drive to the hospital.

For Dash's sake—and for the sake of my own pride as a
professional healer—I hoped that the diagnosis would be confirmed. There was a part of me that quickened to the chase, a
detached intellectual contest that pitted me against unknown
enemies in a battle for Dash's life.

In some ways, making a diagnosis can resemble a mental video game, where threat after threat must be eliminated until you come face to face with the ultimate culprit. Once the cause is isolated through diagnosis, the game moves to a new level. The final battle is joined as you try to find the best treatment to vanquish the disease. In the process, it's easy to forget the love and loyalty that bind pet, owner, and healer together.

I was still caught up in the spirit of this game as I waited eagerly for the results of Dash's consultation at Angell Memorial. Would I be right? Would the neurologist confirm my diagnosis?

A few hours later, the veterinary neurologist called with the news. "It *is* coonhound paralysis," he said.

I had been proven right, but somehow, the knowledge that I could make such a tough, obscure diagnosis felt unfulfilling, hollow. What had been missing from my medical game-playing was a heartfelt response to the pain of Dash and his owner. Sure, I had been right. You could argue I was a clever diagnostician. But now, what could I *do* for the animal? To answer that question, I had to shift the focus from my head to my heart.

There is no magic bullet that will cure coonhound paralysis. The only treatment is simply to wait out the disease through weeks of painstaking nursing care and hope that the paralysis will gradually disappear. It's a commitment that few people are willing to make. Out in the country, when a dog is as sick as Dash was, it's not uncommon for the owner to take him into the backyard and with a single shot put him out of his misery.

Would Bill have the time and patience—and the emotional endurance—to go the extra mile for Dash? If he said yes, it would mean that for the next two or three months his life, Dash's, and mine would be intimately intertwined. We would be walking down an unknown road to healing, and as Dash's vet, I would have to be Bill's guide.

Bill didn't hesitate for a moment. "Dash is all I have," he said quietly.

At home, Bill made a big soft bed for Dash where he could lie comfortably on his side. During the day, Bill rushed home from work every few hours to roll Dash from one side to the other, as I had instructed him. At night, he set his alarm to wake him up so he could shift Dash's position again. As time-consuming as this effort was, Bill had no choice if he wanted to keep his dog alive. Without such attention, Dash might lie on one side too long and quickly develop pneumonia. Frequent shifting also helped ward off bedsores.

Everything that Dash needed was provided by Bill's loving hands. At mealtime, he tenderly held Dash's head in his lap and spooned the food into his mouth. Each morning and again at night, he took Dash outside and held him upright over an appropriate spot on the lawn until he finished his business.

Through such intimacies, Bill and Dash developed a power-ful interdependence that took on a life of its own. Instead of being beaten down by Dash's condition, the two were ener-gized by it, and the routine gave them the needed impetus to make it from one day to the next. With each passing day, Bill's sense of purpose grew. He looked forward eagerly to coming home and taking care of Dash. And Dash reciprocated in the only way he could. His eyes lit up with joy the minute he caught sight of his friend and caretaker.

After only a week, there was a faint sign that something in Dash was beginning to stir. When I stopped by one day to check on the patient and the door slammed behind me, Dash raised his head to see who had arrived.

"Wow" I exclaimed. "He can lift his head up!"

Immediately, he dropped his head back down, worn out by the effort. But this ever-so-slight response was sufficient to generate some excitement. Bill lay down right next to him, with his face touching Dash's, nose to nose. Gently, he stroked Dash's cheek. Dash rallied long enough to stick out his tongue and give Bill a few affectionate licks.

From then on, a sense of expectation permeated Bill's home, and I too became caught up in the air of optimism. Every few days, I dropped by to give Dash a physical and show Bill new techniques he might use to speed his progress. I taught him how to watch for signs of bedsores or dehydration. I even developed a physical therapy program, giving Bill pointers on how to stretch Dash's legs and massage the muscles to increase circulation. If it would help Dash, Bill was willing to try it.

Several weeks passed without much change. Dash was still lying flat on his side, and Bill had to come home every couple of hours to roll him over. But he never complained. Instead, he plied me with questions and became so tuned in to the nuances of Dash's physical condition that he developed a sophisticated eye for medical problems.

Bill's never-say-die determination was rewarded about a month later. Dash was lying motionless on his side as usual—but then he bent his right front leg and slowly stretched it back out.

"Look at that!" Bill shouted. "He's getting better!" Moments later, Dash flexed his left front leg. His hind legs came along a few days later.

It took Dash another month to summon enough strength to stand up. He tentatively got to his feet, and with his whole body shaking from the strain, stood on all fours for a few seconds. Then his legs gave way and he fell back on the bed, where he promptly went to sleep. When he woke up, he tried again. And then again.

Four months from the day I had diagnosed his coonhound paralysis, Dash finally returned to normal. But for Dash and Bill, nothing would ever be the same. In the constant physical act of giving and receiving, they had become as one. Dash, the faithful mutt who loved his master unconditionally, had received that affection and devotion back tenfold. And Bill, who had always been comforted by the quiet presence of Dash, had found in himself a capacity to care that touched some inner recess of his soul.

THE MEDITATIONS OF MARK AND LADY
A Touch That Is Transcendent

Sometimes—as began to happen with Bill and Dash—the healing that accompanies a loving touch may reach far beyond physical contact. This transcendent, even spiritual, dimension flowered in a unique fashion with Lady, a six-year-old Doberman with bone cancer. When Lady was brought in to me for treatment, I must say that the initial outlook wasn't too promising. She was limping, a condition that Mark, the owner, had attributed to a bad sprain until the malignancy was diagnosed. The x-rays revealed that Lady's ankle was encapsulated by a cancerous growth that had caused part of her lower leg to swell by more than an inch.

One veterinarian had recommended that her leg be amputated, but Mark wouldn't hear of it. He worried about the shock that such an operation might have on her system. He was also concerned about the loss in mobility and the possible depression that having only three legs might bring, although the veterinarian had assured him that many animals adapt immediately to being three-legged. Finding some alternative to surgery seemed best for this particular pet and her owner, and that's why they ended up in my office.

I suggested focusing on a diet and supplements high in vitamins, a few homeopathic medications, and also doses of shark cartilage, which some veterinarians believe may help slow the growth of a cancer. But I cautioned Mark that in cases like this, it was best not to get your hopes too high.

"We'll try everything we can," I said. "But I think the *best* treatment would be for you to try to draw even closer to Lady in the weeks ahead. Show your love and concern. Talk to her more. And just *be* with her as much as you can in a calm and peaceful way."

So Mark proceeded to embark on his own personally designed "communion of the spirit" program with Lady. There was no right or wrong way to go about this, except to pick an approach that communicated the genuine love and compassion he felt.

He would sit quietly at home with Lady on his lap, relaxing on his porch in the early evening. That was a time when there was little or no noise outside, no planes overhead, no shouting children in nearby yards, and few cars on the road in front of the house. During those peaceful moments, Mark would say little, but instead would *visualize* the area in the dog's leg that was cancerous. Holding Lady on his lap, he would breathe regularly, picture the inside of that leg, and imagine throwing the cancer away. His approach was similar to that recommended for patients by physicians in mind-body medicine.

Periodically during these special times, Mark would talk to Lady, but he had to discipline himself to focus on the positive, not the negative. If he became doleful or downcast in his words or thoughts, that attitude would invariably be communicated to the dog—and Mark could immediately feel her own uncomfortable or depressed response. So he worked consciously at not allowing his voice to waver or to sound unhappy or despondent.

At first, as Mark visualized and meditated over the dog, the leg with the tumor felt hot to the touch. Then, after a few weeks of positive interactions between them, the heat dissipated, so that the diseased leg felt only somewhat warm. Subsequent x-rays actually showed that the growth of the cancer had stopped. And blood tests that indicate the presence of cancer, such as the level of the biochemical alkaline phosphatase, improved considerably after the spiritual bond between Lady and Mark had intensified.

Also, on a purely emotional level, Lady became more relaxed when they were pursuing their mutual meditation. And she seemed increasingly alert and playful at other times of the day.

Mark would be the first to admit that he couldn't fully explain the physical improvement. The remission that Lady experienced might have been just a natural occurrence in the course of the cancer. Or perhaps the change in her diet, or the use of homeopathic remedies, was the operative ingredient. Although Lady didn't make it in the long run, neither Mark nor I could discount the special emotional union that had developed. In fact, I sensed that something beyond known scientific or physiological factors had been at work.

You can't quantify or analyze love or compassion, but many know how strongly they can influence human emotional moods and physical responses. When the healer really loves, and then communicates that love through touch to a patient, wonderful, unpredictable responses can occur. As the father of medicine, the ancient Greek Hippocrates, once said: "Some patients, though conscious that their condition is perilous, recover their health simply through their contentment with the goodness of the physician."

Dr. Herbert Benson of the Harvard Medical School, perhaps the leading medical authority in exploring mind-body interactions, has put a modern-day spin on Hippocrates' insight by linking it to the placebo effect, or the ability of belief to cause a significant physical response. "The thoughts and behavior of the healer or physician are ... supremely important in the working of the placebo effect," Benson wrote in *Beyond the Relaxation Response*. "Those healers who are attentive to the needs of the patient, who are self-confident and have faith in the effectiveness of their treatments, are much more likely to cause the positive placebo effect to come into play."

If belief and positive feelings can work such benefits between humans, why not between a human and a beloved animal?

I've become convinced as a result of years of veterinary practice that something which encompasses but also transcends the physical is indeed at work in situations like the one experienced by Mark and Lady. Whether we are dealing with some as-yet-undiscovered submolecular wave phenomenon, or with an ingredient of the unified theory that has become the Holy Grail sought by physicists, or simply with an ineffable and unknowable reality, I can't really say. But I do know that something exciting, something beyond our wildest imaginations, is released when we give ourselves over completely to a compassionate touch in love and service to another creature.

CHAPTER SIX

Feeling

Love animals. God has given them the rudiments of
thought and joy untroubled. Do not trouble their joy,
don't harass them, don't deprive them of their happi-
ness, don't work against God's intent. Man, do not
pride yourself on superiority to animals; they are
without sin, and you, with your greatness, defile the
earth by your appearance on it, and leave the traces
of your foulness after you—alas, it is true of almost
every one of us!

—FYODOR DOSTOYEVSKY, *THE BROTHERS KARAMAZOV*

From the very beginning, I sensed there was something peculiar about the dog. She was only a year old, a German shepherd,
little more than an adolescent. Instead of walking into my office
proudly and confidently, as most shepherds do, this one ran in
with her tail between her legs and cowered under a chair. The
minute her owner opened his mouth to speak, the dog sank
down even lower to the floor.

According to the owner, Max, a hulking construction worker
with the biggest biceps I had ever seen, the dog was having
bladder problems. "She wets all over the house," he said. "I tell
her to stop, and she keeps wetting even more. I've tried swat-
ting her. I've tried yelling. Nothing works. It's driving me crazy."

"Okay. Let's take a look at her," I said. And as I started to
talk, the dog, whose name was Rosie, peeked out from under
the chair and sniffed at my leg.

"No!" shouted Max. "Stay still!"

Rosie's eyes filled with fear and she immediately scrunched
up as small as she could underneath the chair.

There was an arrogance and brutishness to Max's voice that jarred me. It didn't take much to suspect that the dog's wetting problems were probably behavioral, not physical. But to be certain, I had to run a number of routine tests. It was possible that Rosie had a congenital problem. A complete urinalysis and battery of blood tests would tell if her kidneys were functioning properly or if she had an infection.

A day later, her tests came back negative, and I was even more certain that Rosie's problem was psychologically induced. Although German shepherds can give the impression of being assertive, this one had been low in the dominance order in her litter, according to her family history. It was quite possible that she was naturally submissive and easily cowed by the tone of her master's voice. As a result she had become what is known as a "passive wetter."

How could I tell Max the truth—that Rosie was cowering and urinating because she was intimidated by him? How could I tell him that for the dog to get well, *he* would have to change?

I told Max that all of Rosie's tests were normal and, finally, I said as delicately as I could, "It might be that she has a behavioral problem."

Max wasn't ready to hear anything that smacked of psychology. "My dog's not a wimp!" he said bluntly. Then he turned to Rosie, and said in an ominous tone, "You're not a wimp, are you?"

At the sound of Max's voice, Rosie's ears dropped back, and from the look of terror in her eyes, I could tell that if I hadn't been in the room she might have been in for a beating.

"There's another test she can take," I interjected quickly, trying to break the tension. "A special type of x-ray will show us if she has any defect in the connection of the bladder to the urethra. I'll have the results in a day or two. Bring her back then and we'll see what we can do."

Unfortunately for me—and for Rosie—her x-rays also proved normal. Now it was up to me to break the news to Max.

As I explained the situation to him, he looked back and forth between me and the dog as though there was some sort of conspiracy between us. "Medically, your dog is fine," I said.

"But from what you've told me about Rosie's personality, it's clear she has a low self-image and needs to be handled more gently."

The scowl on Max's face told me I was venturing into forbidden territory. "I know it may be difficult," I continued, "but you're going to have to act softer and kinder toward Rosie. She seems to be getting the wrong message from your tone of voice. She takes it as disapproval. The only solution is to try to build up her self-image. It'll take a lot of work—but it can be done."

At that, Max rolled his eyes and shook his head. Clearly, a dog as sensitive as Rosie was not his idea of man's best friend.

He sat there for a few moments, bristling inside. Then he stood up abruptly and said, "I don't want a wimpy dog. You can have her." And with that, he turned on his heel and walked out.

Rosie didn't even bother to look up. She just lay there under a chair, head on her paws, until I knelt down and whispered for her to come out. I extended my hand and she stretched out her head and started sniffing.

I patted her on the chest rather than on the head, so I would not appear threatening, and wondered what to do next. I wasn't sorry to see Max go. Although the prospect of filling my hectic schedule with yet another demand didn't exactly thrill me, I was overjoyed to have rescued Rosie from the clutches of a man who only wanted a dog created in his own rough image.

The challenge I faced was to draw out the dog that was buried inside Rosie—the personality that had been beaten down by an abusive and overcontrolling master. It would be a daunting task, but I was determined to give it a try. To lift Rosie's self-esteem would take a limitless supply of patience and love. But I knew that I would have a helpmate—my golden retriever, Megan. During the day when I was at work, she would be able to provide the kindness and nurture that Rosie needed.

That night, I took Rosie home and started her on a crash course in canine confidence building. The minute I walked in the door, Megan bounded over and began to sniff Rosie all over and smother her with affectionate licks. Rosie didn't seem to know what to do. Her eyes darted back and forth nervously as she stood with her shoulders hunched up tight. But after a few minutes, when she realized Megan wasn't a threat, she began to relax. Her body loosened up and she even managed to muster up a few tentative sniffs in return.

Later on, to put the newcomer at ease, I played for a while with Megan and then made a few gentle overtures toward Rosie. I lay flat on my stomach in a nonthreatening pose, and averting my eyes, held out my hand in a gesture of friendship. I knew that if I looked her straight in the eyes that it could be interpreted as a challenge, increasing Rosie's anxiety level and thwarting my efforts to boost her ego.

So I waited. And waited. After what seemed like an eternity, Rosie slowly moved toward my hand and started sniffing. I didn't move a muscle. She kept sniffing, and gradually I was able to lift my hand and start to pet her. All the while, I whispered words of assurance. Megan, meanwhile, stood quietly at the side of the room observing this interaction with what seemed like approval.

The next night, it was more of the same. I played with Megan, hoping to impress on Rosie a model of warm, loving behavior between friends, then I stretched out on the floor and held out my hand to draw her in. Within a few days, I was able to sit cross-legged on the floor with Rosie next to me as I stroked her, whispering words of encouragement and love.

But the picture wasn't all perfect. Some nights I would come home from work exhausted and find that Rosie had urinated in various corners of the house. There were telltale signs in the bedroom, in the corner of the living room, and in the den. My heart would sink as I contemplated the work that lay ahead. Not only did I have a mess to clean up, I also had to face the fact that Rosie's recovery wouldn't happen overnight.

But I couldn't let on what I was feeling. If my voice, eyes, or body language betrayed any trace of disapproval, Rosie would pick up on it immediately. So while I was cringing inside at the smell of urine and the sight of the damp spots on my rug, I always managed to smile and sound upbeat.

"Hi, girls, I'm home!" I would call out enthusiastically. And

Megan would rush over to greet me, followed by a hesitant Rosie. I reached down to pet one, then the other. Then I knelt on the floor and put my arms around them both, giving them a big hug.

What Rosie needed was love, not punishment, no matter how egregious her behavior. If I wanted this dog to become the healthy and happy creature she was meant to be, I had to cling to my faith that one day soon the positive reinforcement I was giving her would pay off.

Finally, I began to see that Rosie's confidence was growing in small ways. After she had been with me for almost a week, I took a chance and looked her straight in the eye when I held out my hand in greeting. Instead of holding back, she came forward to lick my hand in what was for her a supreme act of trust.

Gradually, her bouts of wetting tapered off, and after about two weeks there were no more episodes. And her physical control was a reflection of her newfound confidence. One night when I walked in the door and shouted hello, it was Rosie, not Megan, who was the first to meet me. She ran right over to me with her tail wagging and raised her head to be petted. Our eyes met, and I could see from her enthusiastic greeting that she was a new dog.

"Rosie, you're great!" I exclaimed, squatting down and nuzzling up close. "I'm so proud of you!"

About a month later, I sensed that Rosie was well enough to move on to another family. It couldn't be just any family, of course. If I were to give her up, it would have to be to people who were compassionate and caring, who understood the universal need of anyone—animal or human—for love and encouragement. I found such people in the Bertellis, a wonderful couple with two young children, who embraced Rosie as if she were a long lost member of the family. Their enthusiasm for her was infectious, and only a few minutes into the first visit, it was clear that Rosie had transferred her trust from me to them without any hesitation.

The children loved Rosie immediately, and when the older son threw a stick for her to retrieve, she raced out on the lawn, picked it up in her mouth, and proudly returned it to the boy amidst cheers and applause. To see her like this, with her head held high and her gait sure and steady, it was hard to imagine that only a few weeks before she had been cowering under a chair in my office.

Rosie's situation may have been extreme, but like her, most animals feel deeply, revealing psyches far more complex than we have ever imagined. They may experience joy or sadness, satisfaction or anguish, inner peace or extreme agitation, supreme self-confidence or deep self-doubt. Furthermore, the good feelings can be enhanced, and the bad feelings aggravated, by the nature of their relationship to their special human companion—their owner, the person who is closest to them and most likely to establish a kinship of spirit, a melding of mind and emotions.

Whether we realize it or not, the emotional as well as the physical environment we create has a direct impact on the way our pets behave. Some veterinarians have coined a term for this: it's the "sponge theory," a scientifically unproven yet very real phenomenon that occurs when pets soak up the energy around them and respond accordingly.

Call it vibrations. Call it magnetism. Call it "bio-waves." Whatever the label, we emit energetic signals related to our deepest feelings which are picked up by those around us, especially our pets. Consider this anecdotal evidence:

• A woman going through a difficult divorce made a practice of swimming far out into a cove every day at her summer home off the Maine coast. During her swim, if she went out beyond a certain buoy, her Labrador retriever would plunge into the water and swim out until he was at her side. Then he would grab hold of her until she moved in closer to shore. The following summer, when the strain of the divorce was over, she again went for her daily swim. But this time, no matter how far out she swam, the dog stayed on the beach. His anxiety—and hers—had disappeared.

• Patty was nervous every time she got on her new horse, a fourteen-year-old Appaloosa. She knew he lacked confidence in his ability to run fast and free, and whenever he broke into a canter, his fear took over. He snorted for breath and pulled forward on the reins as hard as he could, straining to go faster and faster. He was so out of control and off balance that Patty's shoulders ached after every ride from the effort of trying to hold him back.

But one day, she decided to make a radical change in her attitude toward her horse. Instead of approaching the Appaloosa warily, she spent a long time relaxing herself with yoga exercises and preparing him for the ride. For an hour, she slowly brushed him down, massaged him, and talked to him. And then just before mounting him, she closed her eyes, put her hands on his neck, and said, "Okay, I'm going to let you carry me."

This time, the ride was like no other. The Appaloosa drank in her sense of calm and confidence and in the process became transformed. When he broke into a canter, he was light and airy and elegant, as his body and Patty's conformed in perfect balance. Together, she said, "we were a new being—like a centaur."

• A pregnant woman discovered that her baby was coming so quickly that there was no time to get to the hospital. She lay down on her living room sofa and went into agonizing labor. All the while, each of her two golden retrievers responded to her pain in his own way. One fearfully ran for cover, quivering in a corner. The other, desperately needing to give comfort, ran back and forth bringing the woman all of his rubber toys—one by one—until they were piled up in a heap next to her body.

All of these animals were expressing deep feelings that were directly related to the environment around them, to the emotional ups and downs of the people they loved. Sometimes, because the animal is so in tune with its closest humans, the feelings are magnified and become manifested as disease. Over the years, I've seen scores of pets who suffered from skin con-

ditions, back problems, behavioral problems, or immunologi-
cal disorders simply because they felt so deeply and had great
difficulty coping with inner problems like a fear of abandonment, anxiety arising from human tensions, or a strong sense
of insecurity about their role in the family.

FACING THE FEAR OF ABANDONMENT

Sandy was covered with a non-contagious form of mange. The
dog, a two-year-old crossbreed, was suffering from an acute
case of parasitic mites that caused itchy, oozing sores on her
skin. These mites live naturally on most dogs and only cause
problems when there's a breakdown in the immune system.

Sandy's problems had started when she was still a canine
"toddler." She had been rescued from a pound when she
was six months old, and just a few weeks later the mange appeared. Her veterinarian had managed to clear up most of the
itchy patches with weekly dousings in a medicated bath, but
her front paws wouldn't respond. The skin between the toes
was so red and ulcerated that the only way to control the pain
was to bandage the paws. The minute the bandages were taken
off, she gnawed at her paws until they became even more
raw.

In search of a cure, Sandy's owners once had driven five
hours to see a veterinary dermatologist at Cornell. But not
even his special dip of mineral oil and insecticide had succeeded in clearing up the disease. "You'll just have to keep her
feet bandaged," the dermatologist said. "There's nothing more
we can do."

For a whole year—half of her young life—Sandy had walked
around with bandaged paws. By the time she showed up at my
clinic for acupuncture, her owners, a flight attendant and her
lawyer husband, were distraught. Sandy was their baby and
they couldn't bear to see her continue in such agony.

It was clear that their love was reciprocated by Sandy. When
the wife left the examining room for a few minutes, Sandy's

eyes followed her and remained transfixed on the door until the woman returned.

As I unwrapped the bandages, I could see the tortured expression on Sandy's face. The pain was so intense that when I lifted her paw to examine her toes she tried to bite me. I knew that though she was generally sweet, the only way I could hope to give her an acupuncture treatment was to muzzle or tranquilize her.

With a muzzle in place, I carefully inserted the acupuncture needles and prayed that they would work their miracles. Although I had had great success using acupuncture for immune problems, Sandy's case was so severe I couldn't be sure of the outcome. Six treatments later, to even my amazement, Sandy was prancing around without pain—and without bandages. All of the ulcers between her toes had cleared up, and the hair had grown back on her paws. Even her coat had a healthy sheen. A microscopic exam showed that there was no evidence of live mites.

Sandy was completely cured, or so it seemed. But a few months later, her owners called with bad news. The mange had returned, not just once, but two or three times since the dog's last treatment. "Why do you think it came back?" I asked, trying to get to the bottom of the problem. "Have there been any changes in your life?"

That was when the real story unfolded. The mange would come back every time the woman was away for more than a week on long airline assignments. Short trips didn't seem to bother Sandy, but when three days stretched into seven or eight, the dog became inconsolable. The woman's husband would find Sandy lying in a corner, her head between her paws. Without the person she loved most around her, Sandy moped about all day and wouldn't eat a thing.

These and similar signals gave me a good idea about what was going on inside Sandy. It seemed fairly clear that she felt abandoned—just as she had as a puppy when she ended up at the pound. And her fear of abandonment may have suppressed her immune system, leaving her vulnerable to an attack of mange.

Although the source of Sandy's problem appeared to be resolved, the question still remained as to what could be done about it. The woman certainly couldn't quit her job with the airline, and she couldn't take Sandy with her on trips. But after she discussed the matter with me and her husband for a while, a light began to dawn. The solution to her dilemma emerged right next door. As it happened, Sandy's owners had an elderly neighbor who loved the dog as much as they did. So the owners and their neighbor were able to arrive at an understanding that seemed to delight them all. Whenever the woman had to be away on a long trip, such as to the West Coast or Europe, Sandy would stay with the neighbor.

With the constant affection and togetherness from her owners and their surrogate, Sandy no longer had reason to fear abandonment. And she never had mange again.

ANTIDOTES TO ANXIETY

The pressures of marital strife and divorce can be communicated to pets, and they may then internalize the tension, expressing their own form of anxiety. An Akita named Kimo gagged every time he tried to eat. Within minutes after he took a bite the gagging would start, and he would regurgitate his food and cough uncontrollably. It didn't happen just once a day, but typically eight or more times. And during each attack, he would go into such spasms that he looked as though he was choking to death. His weight had dropped precipitously, and the gloss had completely gone out of his coat.

When Kimo was first brought to me by his owner, a man in his forties, I had no reason to suspect that his illness might be aggravated by emotional tensions. His condition, known as megasophagus, or paralysis of the esophagus, can be caused by a host of medical problems, including hypothyroidism and myasthenia gravis. But a series of tests for these diseases proved negative, and I was left with a mystery diagnosis: "idiopathic" megasophagus, or megasophagus of unknown causes.

Was there some emotional force, of which I was unaware, that might be triggering the physical symptoms? That suspicion had occurred to me, but in the meantime I proceeded to suggest to the owner possible courses of treatment that could alleviate the paralysis of the dog's esophagus.

I explained to the owner that the conventional medical approach in this case would be to pursue a rather complicated, two-part treatment. First I could give the dog medications to increase the motility of the esophagus. Then I could train him to eat on a ladder with his head raised up. In that way the food would go down the esophagus by the force of gravity. But inevitably, such treatment causes the food not only to go down the esophagus, but also to enter the lungs, possibly causing inhalation pneumonia.

When I explained the dangers of this course of treatment, the owner asked, "How about acupuncture?"

Although I had never used acupuncture in such a case, I was willing to try. I pored over my acupuncture books that night and came up with some acupoints that might control the gag reflex. We started treatment the next day, but I still wondered if there might be an emotional component to Kimo's problems. During the course of my treatments, I noticed that either the owner or his wife brought Kimo to my office; they never came together. And both seemed to be under great stress. If they were having marital problems, it was possible that the dog was internalizing the tension.

After the very first acupuncture treatment, there was some improvement. Kimo was regurgitating three times a day instead of eight. After the second treatment three days later, he coughed up food only once a day. Following the third treatment, he was able to hold down his food consistently and only coughed up a little mucus once a day. With the fourth treatment, he was coughing up mucus only every few days. Two weeks following the first treatment, his coat had become shiny and he looked not only well fed but also full of life.

By any standard, the treatment was a complete success. I also learned that Kimo's owners had separated, perhaps relieving some of the tension that could have aggravated their pet's condition. But just two months later, I was faced with a dilemma that even Solomon couldn't have solved. The phone rang one day and it was the wife. "We've been going through a terrible divorce," she told me. "My husband wants Kimo, and so do I. But neither of us wants the other to have him. So we want you to put him to sleep."

I was dumbfounded. "Can't I take him?" I asked.

"No," she insisted. "He'd still be there as a connection between us. We can't handle that."

In other words, because their human relationship had fallen apart, they wanted to terminate the relationship with their pet as well. Of course, there was no way I could fulfill her request. After all, I had just brought the dog back to life. At eight years old, he was hale and hearty and had plenty of good years left. But my refusal didn't change their minds. They took Kimo to another vet, and in a final coup de grace, put an end to the last tangible link in their marriage.

If Kimo's story is sobering in the intensity of the emotions unleashed, the tale of a sheltie named Truffles holds out more hope of healing, both for pets and the people who own them. Truffles was a typical sheltie, brown and white, with a leonine mane around her face that imbued her with an air of nobility. Owned by a couple in their forties, the dog had come to me for acupuncture to relieve her severe back pain from a slipped disk.

For the first few visits, it was the wife who brought Truffles to the clinic, and she had been overjoyed to see a dramatic improvement in the dog after just one treatment. In between the second and third treatment, Truffles had been without pain —except for two or three excruciating spasms, which occurred under telling circumstances.

"The only time I see an episode of pain is when my husband and I are fighting," the woman admitted, cuddling and cradling Truffles in her arms as she spoke. "It's ironic, but Truffles' problems started when we began to go through a divorce. My husband and I are both alcoholics, and after I stopped drinking through a recovery program, I gave him an ultimatum. He chose alcohol over me. So we're getting a divorce."

Further probing into the connections between Truffles' illness and tensions in the home suggested that the dog was helping to shoulder the wife's anxieties. "I love you so much," the woman said to Truffles one day at the clinic, petting her head. "You're the one who's getting me through this."

In return for the dog's devotion—and in a kind of compensation for the suffering the animal was experiencing as a result of the family upsets—the woman made sure that Truffles would be cared for, no matter what happened to the marriage. It wasn't long after the woman and her husband separated that he brought Truffles to the clinic. "I can't believe my wife wants me to do this for the dog," he said, shaking his head in amusement. "But in our divorce settlement, she's stipulated that I pay for Truffles' acupuncture treatments!"

After the divorce, Truffles was now living in a relatively stress-free environment and was pain-free, although I continued to see her every four months or so as a preventive measure.

OVERCOMING INSECURITY

The stresses of human dynamics can trigger not only anxieties in a sensitive pet but also a profound sense of insecurity about its role in the family. And this insecurity often comes to the surface in such physical symptoms as lesions and other skin disorders. If we are attuned to the underlying source of our pets' problems, their illnesses can sometimes act as a bellwether, a signal that we need to change our family circumstances—for the good of our pets *and* ourselves.

Timothy was a tabby with a raw patch of baldness on his belly where he had licked off his fur. He was brought to me by his owner, a seventeen-year-old girl named Roxanne. She explained that the cat had been treated by another vet with drugs and hormones, but every time she had taken him off the medications, the licking would start again.

I went through the usual litany of questions to see if there were any environmental changes in the house that could have caused Timothy's problem: a new rug, furniture that might have been treated with chemicals, a change of diet—any of the things that can stimulate an allergic response in cats. But each time I ticked off a possible cause, the girl shook her head no.

"Is there any stress in the family that the cat might be sensitive to?" I asked gently.

Roxanne sat silently for a few moments, and then tears started streaming down her cheeks. "My parents are constantly fighting," she confessed. "And . . . I've been abused by my father. He goes into a rage and hits me for no reason. I've noticed that whenever my father or mother starts screaming at me, or when my father threatens me, Timothy goes into a corner and hides. He starts licking and pulling his hair out. And he won't let my father near him. Whenever my dad moves toward him, Timothy hisses at him. He'll swipe the air with his claws to keep my dad away. After that, he'll lick himself some more."

Her father's abusiveness had escalated a few months earlier, Roxanne explained, after he ran into some problems at work. That was when Timothy began licking his belly even more vigorously.

As I heard her story, I tried not to show my alarm. I had really opened a Pandora's box with this one. Here I was in an exam room with nearly a dozen other animal owners waiting to see me, and I had to deal with an abused teenager whose parents were fighting. Her cat's problem was clearly related to what was going on in the home, but I knew there was no way I could resolve the family tensions in fifteen minutes. The situation called for a psychologist or a family therapist or a miracle—not a vet.

But Roxanne gave me an opening that showed she was wise beyond her years. "I feel so bad for my cat," she said. "He's destroying himself for me."

I explained to Roxanne that all the hormones and medications Timothy had been taking had merely masked his emotions. That was why whenever he went off the drugs he reverted to self-mutilation. "Your cat's condition is a signal that he's insecure because of his human environment," I said.

"He may want to help you, but he can't do anything about it. Only you and your parents can resolve the underlying family situation by going for help."

In the interim, there was something I could do to help Timothy deal with his psychological symptoms. I gave him "rescue remedy," a flower extract for stress, and "ignatia," a homeopathic treatment—essentially an extremely diluted plant substance—for the grief he was clearly suffering over the abuse to Roxanne. "Also, be sure to give him lots of love," I said. "He's obviously insecure, and the more you can pet him and let him know how much you care, the better he'll be. But please get some help, at least for yourself."

Two weeks later, Roxanne returned with Timothy for a follow-up visit. As she came in the door, I could tell from her energy and the look on her face that she was bursting with new confidence. "I went to see a counselor, and I feel so much better to be talking to someone," she said. "And just look at Timothy!"

The cat sported stubble where the raw patchy skin had been—the result of the love and the sense of control the girl was beginning to project. Although her parents weren't yet at a place where they were willing to go for help, they were coming closer to understanding how their behavior was affecting Roxanne. But it was Timothy, with his sensitivity to Roxanne and his deep insecurity over her welfare, that had signaled the need for outside help and instigated the beginning of a cure.

Just as this particular tabby became insecure due to mounting family tensions, a South Bronx Doberman named Ivan faced inner turmoil when there was a new addition to his household. Ivan had come to me originally with a case of lick granuloma, a self-inflicted ulceration on his leg that resulted from his licking a scar from an old wound. But it would become clear that his problems ran much deeper than surface wounds.

Ivan and his owner made a fearsome duo. The dog had a black leather collar ringed with half-inch spikes and a massive chain for a leash. The owner, Pico, sported a leather vest and a wristband that matched Ivan's collar. For the past year and a half, Pico had gone from vet to vet trying to find some remedy for Ivan's problem. The only thing that prevented the dog from licking the sore was the bandage that never left his leg. When every other treatment had failed, his latest vet referred him to me for acupuncture.

"I think I'll have to sedate this dog or muzzle him to work on him," I said, sizing up the situation.

"No—I'll just hold on to him," Pico said.

I was wary but didn't feel I could refuse. So, with Pico holding Ivan's head, I inserted the first needle. Ivan growled. I looked at Pico, who shrugged his shoulders and said, "No, Ivan." I inserted another needle, and the dog growled again. "Ivan, no!" commanded Pico.

Eight treatments later, Ivan had stopped growling and his leg wound was completely healed. But after just a few more months, he was back in my clinic again with the same problem. "What happened?" I asked Pico.

"We just had a new baby," he said. "Ivan started licking two weeks after the baby came home."

As tough as he was on the outside, Ivan was soft enough on the inside to have been threatened by the new arrival. Clearly, he was a supersensitive dog that had to be handled with special care. "He's probably always going to be inclined to be a little insecure," I said to Pico. "You're going to have to be alert to identify the potential emotional triggers in your home and then take steps to protect Ivan from them."

So Pico showered excessive attention on Ivan in the next few weeks. He also took special pains to keep him separated from the baby, both to protect the child and to expose the dog to as little stress as possible. These steps successfully reduced Ivan's sense of insecurity. He no longer licked his old wound, and within a year he and the child were getting along famously.

BEYOND EMPATHY

Although many of the animals I've worked with over the years have in a sense been victims of human emotional turmoil, there's another, more positive dimension to the feelings that may be communicated between pets and their owners. Frequently, a sensitive animal seems able to empathize with a troubled person and may actually prove capable of bearing that individual's burdens.

Molly sat at Charlotte's feet, looking soulfully into the young woman's face. Charlotte was crying softly as she had for many days and nights since she began to suffer from the first complications of diabetes. Molly, a husky, was only a puppy, but somehow she understood that Charlotte needed her love and comfort.

Charlotte's feet felt as if they were on fire. She was afflicted with "peripheral neuropathy," a symptom of diabetes in which the nerves of the extremities become overstimulated by abnormal blood sugar levels. What this meant in practical terms was that Charlotte was constantly in pain. During the day, her job as a social worker distracted her from the pain. But at night, the burning sensation was so overwhelming that there was nothing to do but cry.

Always, Molly was there. She wasn't hovering or demanding. The puppy just sat there in front of Charlotte, absorbing her anguish and allowing her to lose herself in the solace of fur as she stroked her pet over and over.

As Charlotte's condition worsened, she and her husband, Tom, were at a loss about what to do next. They went from doctor to doctor, trying to find some relief for the pain. One neurologist even suggested that she have certain nerves in her spinal cord severed to alleviate the problem, but none of the doctors was willing to give her enough medication to control the pain. Until her blood sugar levels were brought under control—a trial-and-error approach with various types of insulin that could take months or years—she would simply have to suffer. The sole saving grace, the last line of inner strength, was that Molly was able to draw close, just at the right moment, ever ready to console and comfort.

It wasn't that Molly was consistently an angel. Whether it was the pressures of Charlotte's illness, the dog's own youthfulness, or some combination of the two, she was so difficult to handle at times that Tom had to resort to strict obedience training. He took her to courses, read up on the subject, and before long managed to check her sporadic bouts of aggressiveness. But Molly was also developing into something of a loner, eagerly forgoing the company of humans for the solitude of the bathroom, where she would lie for hours lost in her own reveries.

Still, she always seemed ready to appear with a different, more caring personality when she sensed that Charlotte needed her. On those occasions, she would keep vigil and watch, her big brown eyes focused only on her mistress. Like a mother who wants nothing but to give to her child, Molly poured out what inner energies she had—despite the fact that, as it turned out, she was suffering herself.

Tom and Charlotte noticed that something was wrong with Molly about ten months after she joined their household. Tom would take her for a walk near their home in Westchester County, and she would end up sitting on the sidewalk, unable to move another step. He would then have to pick her up—all seventy pounds of her—and carry her back home.

Molly's diagnosis was hip dysplasia, a malformation of the hip joints. At the same time, she also suffered from severe growing pains. Her limbs were growing unusually fast, causing her to ache constantly when she walked. After a year, the growing pains seemed to subside, but by then she had developed such severe food allergies—a condition that also afflicted Charlotte—that she would chew her coat in relentless fits to relieve the itching.

Tom threw himself into the task of finding a cure for Molly's multiple ailments—which in an eerie way seemed to mirror his wife's health problems. Over the next few years, he went to more than twelve vets in three states, trying to find someone who could control the dog's allergies and soothe her aches and pains. Helping Molly became a crusade. Tom had lost a sister to cancer and knew that there was no cure for Charlotte's diabetes. But here, perhaps, he could make a difference.

To pinpoint the source of Molly's allergies, he tried rotating her food. He had her blood checked at various labs and analyzed endless printouts of data. He put her on a completely vegetarian diet, cooking all the food himself. With each new vet and each new technique, Molly made small strides toward health. One veterinarian in Texas gave Tom an herbal remedy over the phone at six o'clock one morning. Another taught him to use vitamin supplements. Gradually, through Tom's relentless efforts, Molly's allergies came under control. But the pain in her hips seemed impervious to treatment, and by the time she was five years old she had begun to deteriorate rapidly. Walking became an impossible ordeal, and x-rays revealed that her joints were severely arthritic.

I learned about Molly's history when, finally, Tom's search led him to acupuncture—and to my former clinic in Patterson, New York, Brook Farm Veterinary Center, which I had named after the utopian community founded near Boston by Ralph Waldo Emerson and Louisa May Alcott. Molly responded so well to acupuncture that she was walking around without any pain after the very first visit. After a few more treatments, she began to go for more extended walks with Tom, and before long she was walking two or three miles at a stretch.

As Molly's condition improved, Tom told me, Charlotte's was improving as well. In an odd way, their illnesses seemed to follow parallel paths, and for several years they were on a tandem track toward better health—until tragedy struck.

Charlotte's elderly mother, with whom she had always had a stressful relationship, was suffering from senile dementia and had to be put into a nursing home. The burden of overseeing the administrative details of her care and treatment fell on Charlotte, who had spent a lifetime trying to overcome the emotional abuse she had suffered at her mother's hands. Yet she had no choice but to be the guardian for the woman who had been the source of so much pain.

"I'm not going to make it through this," Charlotte told Tom over and over. For months, she went through her paces in a daze. Some days, the only way she could get by was to put one foot in front of the other and just stay in mindless motion. Her body felt like a coiled spring—so tight it might explode at any moment. Some nights, she found herself weeping uncontrollably for no apparent reason. Although Tom tried to help, even his support and gentle words weren't enough to cut through her distress.

But then there was Molly. She sat quietly in front of her mistress with "listening eyes" that seemed to see and empathize with the emotional wounds of her heart. Molly's wordless presence was enough to put Charlotte at peace.

Then Molly got sick again, suddenly and unexpectedly. One day she was bouncy and perky, and the next morning she collapsed on the floor. Tom rushed her to my clinic, where I discovered a cancerous tumor on her spleen which had hemorrhaged. Immediately I gave her a transfusion and a Chinese herb to help clot the blood, and for the next couple of days Tom nursed her at the clinic. Molly rallied and seemed strong enough to go home. She was too far along for surgery, since the ultrasound had revealed that the tumor had spread rapidly throughout her abdomen. All we could hope for was a few weeks, perhaps months.

But she didn't have that long. A day after Molly returned home, at four o'clock in the morning, Charlotte sensed that something was very wrong. She went down to the room where Molly was sleeping with Tom and found the dog breathing heavily. She cradled Molly in her arms and kissed her between the eyes—an affectionate gesture the dog had always loved. Then Charlotte heard a sound coming from the dog that seemed to her to have a specific meaning: "Take my pain."

In disbelief, Charlotte looked at Molly. The words seemed to come again: "Take my pain."

Molly was dying, and her feelings were so intense that somehow, through some medium, they had been communicated. The dog that could empathize so deeply—that had literally borne her human companion's burdens for the past eleven years—was now asking Charlotte to bear hers.

"I understand," Charlotte said.

A few moments passed and Molly slipped away. It wasn't until a few days later that Charlotte understood more fully what their relationship had meant. Sitting alone in her room, feeling at loose ends and desperately needing comfort, Charlotte sensed something soft touching her skin. Molly's thick fur seemed to envelop her in a cozy warmth. Then she experienced a vision, a view of Molly's face, peering at her with those big brown eyes that spoke only of love.

For years, Charlotte had been longing for a caring mother—someone who, unlike her real parent, would feel her tears, share her joys, and care for her through every trial. "I don't need to look any further," Charlotte told Tom. "I know now that Molly was the only mother I'll ever need."

CHAPTER SEVEN

Letting Go

*Every life has a measure of sorrow. Sometimes it is
this that awakens us.*

—ANCIENT BUDDHIST SAYING

It was late one night near closing time when a woman walked
through the door of the examining room, followed closely by
her husband, who was carrying a very sick English setter. As
the man placed the dog on the examining table in front of me,
I noticed that he and his wife were strangely calm. Despite the
lateness of the hour, there was no sign of alarm, no fearful look
on their faces that would suggest that this was an emergency.

Instead, the two bent over the dog and started stroking her.
Then the wife turned to me, and with a faraway look in her
eyes said, "We've tried everything, and we think it's time to put
her to sleep." But I wasn't ready to jump to conclusions. I had
never examined the animal before and I wasn't about to rush
into euthanasia.

"What's wrong with her?" I asked.

"She's been vomiting constantly," the woman said. "And
she's very depressed. We can hear her telling us that she wants
to go—that it's her time to leave her body."

I could tell from the sound of her voice that the woman had
already made up her mind. She seemed so confident about her
decision that I was puzzled.

"What did your veterinarian say?" I asked.

"We didn't bring her to a vet," the woman said. "We took
care of her ourselves with herbs and things." She explained
that she and her husband were writers who dabbled in healing.

When the dog had become sick a couple of weeks earlier, they had chosen a few herbal remedies they thought might work, and when those had failed to help the dog, they looked in a book and tried some homeopathic treatments.

"We prayed over the dog," the woman said. "We meditated. But nothing has worked. We've tried *everything.*"

Everything, that is, except a thorough physical exam that might have elicited a specific diagnosis.

"Would you mind if I just examined the dog?" I asked, hoping to get to the bottom of the animal's problem.

"Sure, take a look," said the woman. "But I know she's letting go."

It was true the dog wasn't in great shape. She was running a high fever, her mucous membranes were pale, and she was extremely listless. But when I palpated her abdomen, I could feel a huge mass that shifted with each probing of my fingers.

"Has she been in heat recently?" I asked, suspecting that she might have developed an infection. Sure enough, she had been in heat a month earlier and not long afterward she had begun to go downhill. I spread open the dog's vagina and out flowed a thick discharge. The dog's uterus was bloated, and even though there was no time to lose, there was a good chance that with surgery she would pull through.

"I'm confident I can save your dog," I said to the woman. "I can perform a hysterectomy on her and remove the pus-filled uterus. Of course, there's an anesthetic risk in any surgery, but I'm sure I can save her."

The woman looked at her husband, whispered a few words, and then turned back to me. In her eyes was the same faraway look I had noticed when she first walked in. "No," she said. "We really feel she's telling us she wants to die. We want you to put her to sleep."

"But I can *save* this dog," I argued, trying as forcefully as I could to make my point. From what I could tell, the dog wasn't letting go. This was a dog that was just sick.

"It's her time," the woman said simply.

I was on the verge of screaming. Before I did anything rash, I had to excuse myself and go into another room, where I bared my soul to one of the technicians. "What am I going to do?" I said, hardly controlling my anger. "I know I can save this dog, but her owners want me to put her to sleep."

I took a few deep breaths to regain my composure and then I went back into the examining room. "Look," I said to the couple, "if money's a problem, I'm sure we can work something out. I'm willing to adopt the dog—anything to keep her alive. Just sign a release form and I'll take her off your hands."

But they were adamant. "We know she wants to leave this planet," the woman said. "We want to do it here, with her. We want to hold her and pet her when she goes."

I was in turmoil. Every ounce of my being fought against doing the terrible thing they were asking of me. Yet what was the alternative? If I didn't put the dog to sleep, another vet would. It was already late, and that would mean the dog would have to live through another night of suffering before she was euthanized. I made one last stab at persuasion. "Is there absolutely no way I can talk you out of this?" I asked.

"We know what's best for our dog," said the man with finality.

So I did something that would haunt me for years to come. I capitulated and prepared to put the dog to sleep. I filled a hypodermic needle with what is essentially an overdose of anesthesia. It's a painless death and would kill the dog instantly.

The couple stood over the dog, hugging her and repeating words of comfort that resounded like a noisy gong in my ears. "You'll be so much better off," they told her. "We love you."

Gently, I held the dog's right front leg and inserted the needle into her cephalic vein. "Please forgive me," I whispered to her. "I'm so sorry."

The dog sighed deeply, and then it was over. Tears streamed down my face as I looked at the limp setter, all brown and white, and thought of what might have been.

I couldn't sleep that night. Or the next. I would wake up sick to my stomach at 3:00 A.M. and replay the entire incident in my mind, wondering how I had come to such a pass. "Why did I become a vet, if I'm reduced to this?" I asked myself.

I weighed the pros and cons of what I had done from the point of view of the dog, but every time my reasoning came up short. The setter hadn't been ready to die. It was the owners who had made the decision for her. They had tipped the scales in the balance of life, imposing their wills, their need for control, on a creature that was at their mercy. From what I could tell, they hadn't even bothered to ask the dog what *she* wanted. And there *was* a way of asking an animal this question and receiving an answer.

A couple of days later, as I was taking Megan for a walk down the dirt road near my house, I came to a decision. "From this day on," I vowed to Megan, "I'm never putting an animal down unless it tells me it's absolutely ready to go."

As it happened, I was to have many opportunities to commune with my patients about whether their time to go had really arrived—and the answers I received were as varied as the pets themselves.

BUNNY

A Time to Heal

Susan Thompson hailed a taxi on East 79th Street in Manhattan and jumped into the backseat. A fawn-colored rabbit was cradled in her arms. "Take me upstate!" she told the astonished driver. "I have to get to my vet immediately."

I had seen the rabbit, aptly named "Bunny," a few days earlier during one of my weekly visits to the New York Animal Medical Center, where I was then on staff. Bunny had a paralyzed hind leg and trauma to the back, problems that are not uncommon among rabbits. But the prognosis was bleak. Even with acupuncture, the rabbit could live only a few more weeks at best.

Still, Susan was adamant. "I've got to do everything I can to keep Bunny alive," she had told me. And now, after a one-and-a-half-hour cab ride, she was sitting quietly in my office as I administered another acupuncture treatment to her pet.

I wondered what had really brought Susan to me. Certainly, I understood the depth of love people have for their pets. But that didn't fully explain Susan's extraordinary desire to extend the crippled rabbit's life. "How long have you had Bunny?" I asked her as I eased the acupuncture needles into the rabbit's leg and back.

"About two years," she said. "She was a gift from my husband, Bob." And at the mention of her husband, Susan's eyes welled up with tears.

"I understand," I said gently.

With that, her story flooded out. She told me that just a few months earlier, her husband, a lawyer, had died of cancer. He was only thirty-four. Bunny had been his gift to her, and now I could see that the rabbit was her only tangible link to the man she had loved so dearly. In a special way, Bunny was the embodiment of the love they had shared. What's more, at a time when Susan needed comfort and caring, she found in this tiny creature the unconditional love that no one else was giving her.

"My mother tells me I'm crazy, and my mother-in-law says I should let go of the rabbit and get on with my life," Susan said through her tears. "But Bunny is the only one who is being sensitive to *me.*"

She tried to regain her composure, but couldn't. "I shouldn't cry," she said through her sobs.

"It's okay," I assured her. "It's not only okay to cry and to grieve, it's good for you."

Over the next few weeks as we worked together to ease Bunny's pain, the rabbit became Susan's entrée to a world beyond despair. During the week, she did what she could on her own to help Bunny by massaging the rabbit's leg and performing physical therapy exercises. Then in my office on weekends, she would relax along with the rabbit as the acupuncture needles helped extend Bunny's life—if only for a brief time.

"You are doing all you can do," I would tell her encouragingly week after week. "The final result isn't up to you."

With every visit, I could see in Susan a growing strength and acceptance. The extra weeks of life for the rabbit were giving her the time to heal. She wasn't bitter, or even grudgingly resigned to Bunny's fate. She was grateful—grateful for the additional time Bunny was giving her to come to terms with her loss. "Every extra moment I've been with Bunny has provided me another chance to say goodbye to my husband," she told me.

Six weeks after her first cab ride to see me, I got a call from Susan. "Bunny just died," she said. "I wanted you to know that she was right here in my arms and I was petting her. You know, Allen," she said softly, "I can't explain it, but I feel strangely warm inside. Bunny gave me much more than a chance to grieve—she gave me back my life."

The deep healing that Susan experienced was an example of the emotional freedom that can come when we share fully and authentically in an animal's death. Sometimes, however, circumstances can cheat us of the time for such sharing and leave us with only our grief.

SPARKY
A Time to Mourn

I was in between appointments on a day filled with barn calls when the phone rang. "Dr. Schoen, please come quickly!" a woman said, her voice choked with emotion. "My horse fell down a well!"

I dashed out the door into the bitter November cold. It couldn't have been more than 20 degrees. An early snow lay thick on the ground and crunched under my feet as I hurried to my car. Although it was only three o'clock, a grayish pall hung over the day, making it seem much later.

In spite of the condition of the roads, I made it to the woman's farm in less than ten minutes. It was a simple place, with a few sheep and goats and a couple of horses. Out back, not far behind the house, was the well into which the horse had fallen. The woman, a widow named Fern Brown, and a handful of neighboring farmers were huddled around the gap-

ing hole, peering down the shaft and calling out words of encouragement to the horse in an effort to calm him.

"We're here, Sparky!" Fern shouted. "It's okay."

One look and I knew it wasn't okay. The shaft was narrow,
only about five feet across, and even though Sparky had fallen
only about twenty feet down, he was wedged in at an impossible angle. It had been a freak accident. The planks covering the
well were obscured by snow, and when the hefty quarter horse
walked across, they had shattered, and he plunged rear first
into the well.

Above the frigid water, all you could see was his head and
his two front legs flailing helplessly in an effort to free himself.
He was terrified. His eyes bulged with the strain, and his facial
muscles were taut with fear. His breathing was coming so hard
and fast it seemed that his lungs would burst.

At the sight of him, I became very quiet, almost withdrawn.
Hope was fast draining out of me. But it was Sparky's horrific
whinny—a piercing shriek that shattered the silence—that
chilled my heart. I had an empty feeling in the pit of my stomach. My whole body suddenly grew cold, clammy. I wanted to
cry along with him as I imagined myself trapped, exhausted,
and panic-stricken, at the bottom of that well.

What could I possibly do to save him? I took a deep breath to
compose my thoughts. Then I gathered Fern and her neighbors
together to try to come up with a plan. One possibility was
to tranquilize Sparky or put him to sleep. But no one had a
tranquilizer gun, and any attempt to reach down into the well
and give him an injection was too dangerous. Although he was
clearly getting tired, he was still striking out with his front feet,
which could kill with one blow to the head.

Another idea was to put a rope around him, attach a tractor
to the other end, and pull him out. That seemed like a pretty
good plan. So first, we jerry-rigged a rope with padding around
it. Then we tried every way we could think of to put a lasso
under his front legs and over his head behind the withers,
which is the space between the neck and the back. That way,
the rope would be supported and we wouldn't strangle him to
death as we pulled. But every time we tried to toss the lasso

over his head, Sparky's front legs waved even more frantically, dashing any hope of success.

By now, more than forty-five minutes had passed, although it seemed we had been at the rescue attempt for hours. So many false starts. So little luck. And with each passing minute, Sparky was getting visibly worse. The energy was draining out of his eyes, and any fight that was left in him was quickly being dissipated.

A wave of nausea swept over me. I actually began to *identify* with Sparky, and at times it seemed that I was stuck in the well myself. My body began to weaken along with his, as the bone-chilling cold and the intensity of the rescue effort took their toll. But I couldn't quit. Even though I was almost certain of the outcome, I dipped desperately into what reserves of strength I had left to keep the rescuers moving forward. I just couldn't let Sparky slip away into an agonizing death in the frigid water of that shaft. He deserved better.

"Let's give it another try," I urged the farmers.

By this time, Sparky was so weak that when the lasso was thrown over him again, he barely moved in protest. The padded rope slipped easily over his head and forelegs, and we were finally able to maneuver it around his withers. One of the farmers hooked the rope to a hoist attached to a tractor, and slowly Sparky was raised out of the well. For a moment, he hung suspended in the air, until his sagging body was lowered onto an old gray blanket that Fern had spread over the snow. And as soon as he was safely on the ground, Fern ran over and pressed up against him, hoping that the warmth of her body would penetrate deep within his.

For the worn-out rescuers, shivering in the cold, the sight of Fern and Sparky, safe at last from the well, brought contented nods of satisfaction. There was a palpable sense of relief that the ordeal was over.

I walked over to Sparky, squatted down, and gently checked him over. He was alive—but just barely. His body was like ice, and he was in such a state of shock that his gums were milky white. The faraway cast to his eyes told me that his mind had already drifted into semiconsciousness.

"What can we do?" Fern asked hopefully, her arms still wrapped around Sparky's neck.

At the sound of her voice, Sparky took a deep breath. Then, with a sigh, he died.

Fern was so stunned that all she could do was clutch his mane and whisper, "Oh dear, oh dear."

Nobody else said a word. What *could* you say after struggling so hard to get the horse out of that well, only to have tragedy strike within minutes of triumph? I looked at the farmers and saw mirrored in their faces the same anguish I was feeling. They were deathly white. Not even a flicker of emotion was left in their eyes. They were spent. Exhausted by the emotional roller coaster they had just been on.

We all stood around quietly for about ten minutes, paying our silent respects to Sparky. I felt helpless and alone, as though I had lost someone close to me. Sparky was just an old quarter horse—one I hadn't even known until that day. Yet, in the hour or so of helping him fight for his life, I had become part of his circle. I had felt his suffering. And now, I was feeling his death as well.

Managing to sum up some degree of detached professionalism, I offered Fern a few words of comfort. I could hear myself saying things like "We did everything that could be done" and "The rest wasn't up to us."

Fern responded not to my words, but to the ache she perceived inside me. What meant the most to her, she said, was that I had been there for Sparky. I had arrived at the farm within minutes of her call. I had poured myself into the futile task of trying to extricate him from the well. Even more important, she said, I had cared about the horse as though he were my own. Through my compassion and love, she felt free to let him go. And now everything would be all right.

The neighbors had already begun to dig a grave for Sparky as I pulled away from the farm and headed back to the office. In the past, I might have tried to forget the whole incident and press on to the next animal, the next disease, without so much as a backward glance. But this time was different. By allowing myself to respond inwardly to Sparky's pain, I had left a piece of myself back at Fern's farm. I knew that giving rein to my emotions wasn't strictly "professional." But I sensed that without the freedom to feel and to mourn for my patients, I could never become the vet I wanted to be.

My experience with Sparky became a watershed event for me in understanding my own emotional responses to my patients. As I mourned, I came to realize that showing we care deeply about our animals isn't just an indulgence, but a necessary part of our humanity.

ALI
A Time to Embrace

She was a Thoroughbred, a regal twenty-six-year-old bay mare with a white star on her forehead. Her owner, Andrea Eastman, had bought her sixteen years earlier and named her Ali after her best friend, the actress Ali MacGraw.

Andrea loved nothing better than to ride Ali for hours on the beach near her home in Malibu. At low tide, the two of them could be seen silhouetted against the setting sun, galloping the whole length of the beach. Then Andrea would dismount and they would walk back toward home, splashing along the ocean's edge.

Nothing was too good for Ali. When Andrea moved from California to the East Coast, she had the horse flown to her new home. Always, Andrea would touch her, massage her, kiss her—anything to let Ali know how much she was loved. And Ali reciprocated, nuzzling Andrea's neck and resting her head on Andrea's shoulder.

Andrea knew Ali needed an overdose of caring. From the very beginning, the horse had been "head shy," hating to have anyone touch her ears. It was a sign, perhaps, that she had been "ear-twitched" for restraint or beaten on the ears by a previous owner who had tried to make her run faster. Whatever the reason, whenever Andrea had tried to bridle her, the horse would toss her head high and out of reach. But, slowly, through her love and caring touch, Andrea developed a technique that overcame Ali's fears. She would stand on a stepladder and gently place the bridle over the horse's head. As Ali came to trust her, Andrea found she no longer needed the ladder. Ali would lower her head to accept the bridle—but only from Andrea.

A few years ago, Ali began to develop a stiffness in her back, the vestige of a trailer accident years before. That's when I first saw her for acupuncture. I treated the horse for about three years, making it possible for her and Andrea to continue their happy rides. The change in Ali was so dramatic that Andrea referred others to me for treatment, including her friend Richard Gere's twelve-year-old Appaloosa, Drughpa, which means "wise man" in Tibetan. Drughpa responded immediately to the treatment.

But with Ali, the acupuncture wasn't a cure-all for her ills, and by the time the horse was twenty-five, Andrea knew it was kinder to retire her. She bought a new horse—a chestnut quarter horse named Indy—and boarded the two animals at a stable near her home. There, the old horse could graze in beautiful green pastures, and Andrea could see her at the barn whenever she came by to ride Indy. As ever, she would walk up to Ali and stand right under her, and Ali would put her head on Andrea's shoulder in a warm embrace.

Their love was so strong that Andrea did everything she could to avoid hurting Ali's feelings. When she rode Indy, she went out the back door of the barn and tried to skirt the field where Ali liked to run so that Ali wouldn't see them. But one day, as Andrea came back from a ride, she noticed out of the corner of her eye that Ali was grazing in a nearby field.

As if by telepathy, Ali immediately picked up her head, trotted over to the fence, and leaned across to touch her nose to Indy's in a kind of horsey handshake. Indy was usually feisty and aggressive around other horses, but that day she was uncharacteristically quiet and respectful. She didn't try to nip playfully at Ali. Instead, she allowed Ali to nuzzle her, and for several minutes the two horses stood nose to nose in rapt communication.

When she had finished this intimate interlude with Indy, Ali looked up and gazed directly into Andrea's eyes—a long, lingering look filled not with reproach, but with gentleness and kindness. Then, she gave a little nod, turned her head, and slowly walked away.

Andrea wanted to cry out, to call Ali back and try to recapture something of those spirited outings in the past which had done so much to cement their friendship. But suddenly she knew that wasn't necessary. Tears welled up in her eyes as she grasped the fullness of what Ali had just done.

"She was letting me go," Andrea said when she described the incident to me. "She had told Indy to take care of me, and then she set me free."

Andrea didn't know it then, but Ali was saying goodbye. Not long afterward, on a beautiful early September evening with a crispness in the air that hinted of fall, she returned from a trip to find that Ali had just fallen ill. The horse had spent a carefree day in the field, running and grazing as she always had. But by nightfall, she was hanging her head and refusing to eat.

By the time Andrea arrived at the barn, Ali's extremities were cold and she was running a fever. Her belly had swelled up enormously, and she seemed to be in great pain. The local vet came at once and examined the horse thoroughly. Then, as gently as she could, she told Andrea that there was nothing she could do. Ali had a tumor, which had grown so quickly that no one had noticed its presence until that moment. At this point, the vet advised, the only humane decision was to put her down.

For about twenty minutes, Andrea stood beside Ali, telling her how much she loved her and thanking her for all the good times they had shared. For a brief moment, her words seemed to cut through the horse's pain. Ali leaned her head against Andrea's and rested it there in a last embrace. Their cheeks were still touching as Ali drifted off into a coma. Andrea put her arms around Ali's neck and stroked her head as the vet administered the lethal injection. Slowly Ali sank to the ground and laid her head down forever.

Some people avoid the presence of death, even the death of a loved one. But Andrea saw Ali's last moments as an invaluable opportunity—a final communion sealing a long and happy companionship that could now continue in spirit, even if not in the flesh.

ROMEO
A Time to Keep

Jacques dropped by my house one day to chat, but after a few minutes it became clear something more than idle talk was weighing on his mind. As a successful designer and art dealer, Jacques had learned quite well how to keep his work and home life in order. But on this occasion his concern wasn't about business or family.

"It's about Romeo," Jacques said, with obvious strain in his voice as he petted his twelve-year-old pug. The dog was lying next to him on the couch and appeared to be on his last legs —literally. For years I had been treating him with Chinese herbs and acupuncture to help his wobbly hind legs, and he had been doing remarkably well. But he was also deaf and had glaucoma, and had lost the use of one eye. Now it looked as if his other eye was in trouble. He had scratched it, and it had become inflamed and was obviously very painful.

"The veterinary ophthalmologist said if it didn't improve with the medication she gave me, we'd have to remove the infected eye," Jacques told me. "He's too far gone for transplants. What do I do?"

I knew that Romeo *lived* to be with Jacques, and vice versa. In fact, the two were inseparable. At night, the dog even slept with Jacques and his wife. And during the day, Jacques carried him everywhere—to his galleries, to friends' homes, to the supermarket. Wherever Jacques went, Romeo went.

But that togetherness had begun to pose problems. In the first place, Romeo was having trouble sleeping. He would start panting in the middle of the night, and the sound got so loud that Jacques and his wife couldn't get any sleep. They solved that problem temporarily by laying the dog on a heap of Jacques' clothing outside the bedroom. That way, Romeo could smell Jacques' scent and feel secure enough to sleep peacefully.

The next problem was a bit thornier. Jacques told me he had several important family gatherings in Paris and in San Francisco that he couldn't miss, and that put him in a bind. He knew he couldn't go without the dog, or Romeo would be devastated. But could he take Romeo to Paris—to his in-law's anniversary party—when the dog had so many physical problems that needed attention? Could the dog survive the trip?

I understood what Jacques was asking. Without really putting it into words, he was asking me whether Romeo's time had come.

"Jacques, some issues are black and white, and some are gray," I said, choosing my words carefully. "Obviously, if Romeo's deaf, becomes completely blind, isn't walking, and is in pain, that's black and white."

"True," Jacques replied. "I know I wouldn't remove the eye if it came to that. I'd put him to sleep. But it seems to me his eye is beginning to heal. He can see shadows again. He's not bumping into things like he used to."

Jacques was obviously looking for reasons to hold on to Romeo for as long as he could. He had already decided to take the dog to Paris, or not go at all. He was even willing to drive with Romeo to San Francisco, he said, if the plane trip might be too stressful. Clearly, here was a man who wasn't yet ready to let go and was showing signs of considerable stress. He started to cry. "What do I do?" he asked me again.

"You need to ask Romeo," I said simply.

Jacques was a clear-thinking businessman who talked straight and didn't have much use for fuzzy thinking. But he understood instantly what I meant. He nodded his head in assent.

"The bottom line is that there's a special connection between you and Romeo," I continued. "You need to talk to him, and even though he can't hear a thing, he will still listen at some level. I can't explain it, but the two of you have been together so long that you have a kind of communication that extends beyond words and beyond hearing. So ask him if it's his time to let go, and he'll tell you."

Jacques didn't need to say a word to Romeo. The dog suddenly started pawing his leg vehemently. Romeo had been practically inert during our whole conversation, but at that moment something jolted him awake.

"This is what you're talking about!" Jacques said excitedly. "This is his answer! He's saying this is not his time, at least not yet."

And that indeed did seem to be Romeo's message. He was insistent that he be allowed to go on living. He was not ready to leave this life. And with that, Jacques scooped up Romeo in his arms and started hugging him. If he needed any more confirmation, he got it again from Romeo, who continued to paw at his arm.

Whether the two of them would have only a few weeks, a month, or several years, it didn't really matter. Jacques knew that he and Romeo would continue for a time to share in the enjoyment of each other's company. In the words of the Preacher in Ecclesiastes, it was their "time to keep." And when that time had passed, Jacques would ask Romeo again, and the dog would let him know.

PART III

HEALING

CHAPTER EIGHT

The Mystery of the Needle

It is better to know some of the questions than all of the answers.

—JAMES THURBER

Just *mention* acupuncture and you'll cause violent debate in the medical community.

A few years ago, I was giving a lecture on this ancient Chinese art and science to some other veterinarians at a major veterinary hospital. We were focusing on one acupuncture point—called "Governing Vessel 26," or GV26—which is located in the center of the space between the nose and upper lip. It is a very important "acupoint," or one of the many spots lying just beneath the skin which can produce significant healing when they are stimulated with a needle or similar device. I've often said that if you and your pet were stranded on a desert island and you had knowledge of only six acupoints, this would be the most important.

The reason why GV26 is so significant is that when stimulated, it increases the body's production of adrenaline (epinephrine), the "fight or flight" hormone that, in turn, stimulates the heart and respiration in times of stress. This spot on the upper lip can be the key to countering cardiac arrest in both humans and animals (see the quite endearing dog and cat illustrating GV26 on page 147). In fact, I believe that every emergency room physician and technician should be familiar with GV26 and know how to make use of it. But with that audience of veterinarians, I went a little further than I usually do when addressing a scientific gathering. I actually said that an animal could suffer cardiac arrest and lose all vital signs and yet might be brought back to consciousness by stimulation of that one acupoint.

A predictable reaction occurred just after I finished my talk. A longtime adversary of mine, a prominent veterinary surgeon, was the first to buttonhole me. "You know, Allen," he said, "I *might* be induced to believe that, once in a while, acupuncture *might* relieve some mild pain in an animal. But I don't want to hear any nonsense about medically borderline methods bringing animals back from the dead!"

"I didn't say we've brought them back from the dead," I protested. "I just said that stimulating this particular acupoint can be a helpful tool if you have an animal that's in cardiac arrest because of the sympathomimetic reaction."

"I don't want to hear this!" he shouted, and turned abruptly away.

The other vets in the vicinity grew quiet, apparently in deference to their colleague. I felt so small. I wished I could just walk out of that hospital and never have to return. But I was scheduled to visit a friend who worked in the emergency room, and so I gritted my teeth and resolved to hold my head as high as possible.

When I reached the emergency room, my colleague patted me on the shoulder and said, "Don't worry, that surgeon always acts that way. He likes to put people down and be intimidating."

It didn't make me feel much better to know that I was only one of a long line of the surgeon's victims. But then fate intervened. At that very moment, emergency technicians rushed in a twelve-year-old German shepherd suffering from life-threatening postoperative complications after surgery for removal of the spleen.

The dog had gone into cardiac arrest. His heart had stopped completely, and no matter what emergency resuscitation procedures the nine veterinarians on the case tried, they couldn't revive him. They tried "intubation" by inserting a tube down the dog's throat. They tried manual CPR by pounding on his chest. They administered injections of epinephrine and bicarbonate. They even attached electrodes to the dog's body and used electric shock in an effort to get the heart started again. They did all the things you are supposed to do to revive a dog whose heart has stopped beating—but to no avail.

After four or five minutes, the veterinarians on the case began to leave the intensive care room one by one. Behind them, the dog's electrocardiogram traced a flat line. The technician handling the artificial respiration was ready to cut off the oxygen being fed to the dog's brain and tissues. The dog's life was virtually over.

"Do you mind if I give it a try?" I asked respectfully.

My presence had gone unnoticed until then. So my question, which shattered the silent air of dejection, was jarring. The few vets still in the room glared at me.

"Sure. The dog's dead. Feel free," one of them said.

I just happened to have an acupuncture needle with me—part of my show-and-tell routine during the lecture I had just delivered. So as the artificial respiration continued, I walked over to the lifeless dog and applied my needle at point GV26—the very location between the nose and upper lip that I had lectured about. The method I used was a kind of "henpecking" technique that involves a series of short jabs to the cartilage, an approach designed to result in much greater stimulation than the usual twirling of an inserted needle.

As I labored, the seconds dragged by, but nothing happened. Just my luck, I thought. Here was the perfect opportunity to prove my point to my colleagues and the technique was failing me.

But then, almost imperceptibly, the dog's chest began to move on its own. There was no doubt about it. The dog was breathing! And I had done it with my needle.

"He's breathing," yelled the technician managing the artificial respiration.

Everyone's eyes turned to the EKG. Now, instead of a flat line, there were jagged, up-and-down movements on the tracer. The dog's heart was beating again!

The other veterinarians in the room appeared to be in shock. Quite literally, their mouths dropped open. Then they rushed back to the dog's side to stabilize his vital functions.

Having heard the commotion, the surgeon who had given me such a hard time earlier in the day put in an appearance. "What's going on here?" he demanded.

One of the other vets, who had performed resuscitation procedures on the animal, tried to explain. "Well," he said, "the dog arrested. There was no heartbeat. It died. We tried everything we could think of, including electric shock. But nothing worked. Then Dr. Schoen came over and stimulated that acupuncture point he talked about earlier today, and the dog came around. It's all recorded on the EKG."

I don't think I actually heard a "harrumph!" But that seemed to be the message in the look the surgeon shot at me just before he stormed out.

Today, I encourage technicians at animal hospitals to learn the GV26 technique. The only difference between my method and theirs is that I use an acupuncture needle, while they may use a small-gauge hypodermic needle to stimulate the spot if an acupuncture needle isn't handy. But acceptance remains atypical. The procedure continues to be regarded as a very new, unfamiliar, and suspect technique in the medical establishment. Sometimes, I get the impression that it's necessary to hit doctors and veterinarians over the head with a genuine, 24-karat miracle that simply *cannot* be denied before they will believe.

One time when I was delivering a talk in Ohio, a veterinarian came up to me and said he had a story to relate that he thought might be of interest. He told me that a colleague of his had returned from Florida about a month earlier, where he had heard an expert on veterinary acupuncture—a certain Dr. Schoen—speak about acupoint GV26. A few days later, this vet's colleague had to treat a dog in cardiac arrest, and unable to revive the animal, he decided he had nothing to lose by trying to stimulate acupoint GV26—which he did with a needle. The dog promptly revived and was stabilized.

But the story didn't end there. The veterinarian was so excited about the outcome that at dinner that evening he related what had happened to an M.D. friend, an emergency room physician. Just as the veterinarian finished his dog story, the physician was beeped and had to rush to the hospital. A little boy had fallen through the ice on a pond and had gone into hypothermia and cardiac arrest. When the doctor got to the hospital, he discovered that the emergency room team had tried every possible means to resuscitate the boy, without success. The doctor took one look at the boy and thought, "Why not?" After jabbing gently with a needle at GV26, he saw the boy come around.

As I deliver lectures on acupuncture around the world, I can never be sure just how far the beneficial ripples will travel. But I *can* be sure that despite my emphasis in lectures on the scientific basis for acupuncture, there will be an occasional challenge from a traditionally trained veterinarian who still questions the validity of the technique. For that matter, I began as something of a skeptic myself—until personal experience and a growing body of scientific studies convinced me otherwise.

BLACKIE'S REBIRTH

It seemed almost too simple when I first heard about it. In fact, the idea bordered on absurdity: that inserting a few copper and steel needles into a dog or horse might mean the difference between health and sickness, or even life and death.

My first brush with acupuncture came during a weekend seminar in a Manhattan hotel. I had shown up for the course merely to get some credits to maintain my New Hampshire veterinarian's license. But at the time, I was also becoming frustrated with some of the limitations of medicine and surgery and hoped that the seminar might offer new insights.

Did it ever. I found myself face-to-face with an extraordinary approach to healing that would change my life permanently.

"If *half* of what you said about acupuncture is true, there's no telling how many animals we can help," I told the lecturer, Dr. Sheldon Altman.

Shelly, a reserved, conservatively dressed Orthodox Jew from Hollywood, California, who is one of the pioneers in veterinary acupuncture, smiled a knowing smile and gave me some practical words of assurance *and* warning: "It's all true, and you're absolutely right—there's no limit to the creatures that can be helped. But if you don't go back to your clinic on Monday and start using these techniques *now,* you'll never do it."

I didn't need any extra motivation. I was already tantalized by the fundamental promise of acupuncture in that the body's own natural healing mechanisms could be used to bring about recovery. What's more, I was currently treating a patient that might benefit: an eleven-year-old Labrador retriever named Blackie. The dog was in such excruciating pain from arthritis that his owner was ready to put him to sleep—unless a miracle intervened.

"Maybe I've found the miracle," I thought.

As soon as I returned to New Paltz, New York, where I was then in practice, I asked that Blackie be brought to my office. For the previous six months I had been seeing him monthly, administering cortisone and pain-relieving medications in an effort to control the inflammation around his elbows, hips, back, and knees. His condition was so serious that x-rays had revealed masses of degenerative, calcified tissue resembling wads of cotton around every joint.

For a while, the medicine had seemed able to control his pain. But now, not even an injection of steroids could relieve his misery. Whenever he tried to walk, he would collapse on the ground and remain where he had fallen, a quivering, anguished mass of black fur. All night long Blackie would cry out in pain. His only hope seemed to be acupuncture.

"I have no idea if this will work or not," I told his owner. "But I've just taken a seminar, I've got twenty needles, and I have these acupuncture maps. How about it?"

"Go for it," he said. "We have nothing to lose."

I put Blackie on the examining table, and with my anatomy

books and acupuncture maps spread out in front of me, I prepared to insert my first needle into a live animal.

Getting started took considerable courage. During the seminar, I had practiced only on oranges! Shelly Altman had assured me that the technique was the same, but still, I didn't want to take any chances. So I probed very carefully and deliberately with my fingers to try to identify the precise points that were prescribed for arthritis and for hip dysplasia.

Using a ruler, I calibrated the exact distances of the acupuncture points, which are located near the elbow and hip joints. Then I checked my calculations and maps again. And again. If the procedure is performed correctly, acupuncture doesn't hurt the patient. But missing the proper location by even a centimeter can result in some discomfort, and I certainly didn't want to inflict any more pain on Blackie than was necessary.

Finally, the technician who was helping me lost patience. After about twenty minutes of watching me probe and ponder and analyze the maps, she said in exasperation, "Will you just stick him with the needle!"

So I took a deep breath and slowly inserted my first needle near Blackie's hip at a key trigger point. The needle went in smoothly. Even though there was a slight muscle quiver, Blackie didn't wince. He actually seemed to relax a little almost immediately.

Following the maps that Shelly had given me, I placed another needle at a point on his back and still another halfway down his leg. Before long, Blackie resembled a porcupine, with needles protruding at 90-degree angles from twenty places along his back, in his hips, and down the upper part of his legs.

I had surprised myself even more than the technician or the dog owner. If someone had asked me how Blackie would react to being punctured in so many places, I would have predicted without any question that he would turn into a squealing, squirming, absolutely crazed canine. Instead, you would have thought he had been given a sedative. After the second or third needle, his eyes began to close, and before long he drifted off into a blissful sleep.

After about fifteen minutes, I removed the needles from his body, as Shelly Altman had instructed during the seminar. Then I roused Blackie and placed him carefully on the floor. There were no barks or whines—but there wasn't really a dramatic change in his condition either. He still walked with a stiff-legged gait, though he did seem to be experiencing less pain in his movements.

"Let's not expect any big change in him immediately," I told his owner, mouthing the cautionary words that Shelly had suggested that I use with an animal owner. "We should go through about eight treatments and only then make a judgment."

We continued the treatments twice a week, and I wasn't sure there was any particular improvement. Blackie seemed to be walking more easily. He seemed to wag his tail more. He seemed to be showing fewer signs of pain. But I was afraid I might be talking myself into a cure that wasn't really happening.

Then came the seventh treatment. When I opened the door for Blackie's visit, he actually *bounded* up to me. Next, he quite literally started to *prance* around my office. His owner followed him with a huge grin. "After the sixth treatment, he slept through the night comfortably for the first time in months," the man reported. "No whining at all. And he's started to play with me again."

When they had left my office, I immediately called Shelly Altman and exclaimed, "It works! It really works!"

Subsequently, I reduced the number of Blackie's treatments to one a week, then one every other week, then once a month, and finally three or four times a year. Needless to say, Blackie was a new dog.

And I was a new vet. With Blackie's recovery, my eyes were opened to an exciting, exotic world of healing that I was impatient to explore. Over the next few months, I devoured everything I could about acupuncture's fascinating historical, philosophical, and scientific underpinnings. I discovered that the procedure dates back thousands of years, originating somewhere in ancient China, India, or Tibet. The discipline became an important part of traditional Chinese medicine, and anthropological evidence shows that veterinary acupuncture was practiced in China as far back as the Shang dynasty, from the sixteenth century to the eleventh century B.C.

Pictures have survived from those long-ago days showing Chinese warriors using arrowheads to stimulate horses to give them more energy prior to battle, possibly through the release of adrenaline. The understanding evolved that by stimulating certain points on the animal's body, you could fine-tune his internal bodily mechanisms, release energy blockages, and prevent, treat, or cure many different diseases.

Much of the theory of acupuncture was based on redressing the balance between what Chinese call yin (the principle of deficiency, coldness, and passivity) and yang (the principle of excess, heat, and aggressiveness). If yin and yang are modified in the optimum way, according to the theory, the body's life force, or *chi,* will be brought into balance, and good health will be maximized. This life force has many corollaries. In Indian medicine, it is called *prana;* in homeopathy, the "vital force"; and in Western medicine, the "bio-electric current."

Using needles, heat sources, herbs, or various forms of pressure, veterinary medicine developed in China into a complex mode of treatment and was finally designated as a separate branch of medicine between 1100 and 770 B.C. The first Chinese textbook of veterinary medicine, which featured acupuncture techniques, was published in 650 B.C.

But centuries passed before these techniques took hold in the West. In the first reported use of the method in Europe, acupuncture was performed on a horse in 1828. For another century and a half, however, the technique remained a relative rarity in Western medicine. Then the situation changed dramatically when President Richard Nixon opened the door to China in the early 1970s.

In those days, the tremendous exchange of art, music, science, and other cultural knowledge also included the introduction of concepts of veterinary acupuncture to the United States. Dr. Shelly Altman had been one of the first people to meet with Chinese acupuncture specialists at UCLA during this period. Soon afterward, expert studies on the subject began to proliferate—and classically trained vets like me were startled by healing possibilities that we had never been taught in school.

IS ACUPUNCTURE GOOD SCIENCE?

In recent years, Western scientists have determined that the acupoints, identified long ago by the Chinese, actually mark the locations of important microtubules beneath the skin, which house tiny nerves and blood vessels. When a needle is inserted through the skin near any of these tubules, a sensory nerve ending is automatically stimulated—and amazing things can happen to stop pain or promote healing.

Furthermore, these acupoints are linked together into lines or "meridians" on the body, which correlate closely to the body's nerve pathways. It seems that electrical charges at several locations along these pathways can promote healing even more effectively.

How exactly does the stimulation of acupoints result in healing and prevention of disease? Scientific research has suggested several possibilities. For one thing, it appears that acupuncture releases endorphins, the morphinelike neurotransmitters that relieve pain and make you feel good. The procedure also releases ACTH, which stimulates the body's internal cortisone, helping to relieve pain and inflammation naturally, without the side effects of drugs.

In addition, applying acupuncture may cause a beneficial microtrauma to the surrounding tissue, causing the release of biochemicals that enhance the immune response and also help fight inflammation in the body. Studies have found that inserting needles into acupoints can actually inhibit pain by blocking certain nerve pathways, and that the use of acupuncture in one part of the body can cause the relaxation or contraction of muscles in other areas. Acupuncture may also stimulate nerves that help relieve diarrhea, constipation, and a variety of other ills.

Although I had witnessed many of these factors at work with Blackie, I soon learned that my first experience with acupuncture was not unique. It was part of a growing body of clinical and research findings that have been able to establish specific scientific links between the art of Chinese acupuncture and Western veterinary medicine. Here are some highlights.

• In 1986, I conducted a study with sixty-five dogs who were so arthritic they had been recommended for euthanasia. They had been treated in all the conventional ways, but without success. Before performing acupuncture, I established four categories to measure the results.

"Unsatisfactory" meant they had no response or such poor response to the acupuncture that they were still candidates for euthanasia. "Fair" meant they improved by more than 25 percent in mobility, energy levels, and overall health. "Good" indicated that they showed greater than 50 percent improvement. "Excellent" was reserved for those that experienced greater than 75 percent improvement. In the "good" and "excellent" categories, the dogs could walk up and down stairs, play easily, jump up on a bed, or perform other vigorous tasks.

After I treated the sixty-five dogs in my study for several weeks with acupuncture, 84 percent—all of which had previously been recommended for euthanasia—improved by more than 25 percent, and 70 percent showed greater than 50 percent improvement!

• In a 1989 study conducted in Belgium by Dr. Luc Janssens, 191 dogs with slipped disks were divided into four groups. Group 1 were hunched up in pain. Group 2 were suffering from pain and nerve damage. Group 3 were completely paralyzed and in pain. And Group 4 experienced paralysis but little apparent pain.

After only four weeks of acupuncture treatment, the investigators found improvement in 94 percent of those in Group 1 (those hunched up with pain), in 89 percent of those in Group 2 (those with pain and nerve damage), in 79 percent of those in Group 3 (those with complete paralysis and pain), and in 20 percent of those in Group 4 (those with paralysis but little pain).

• At the Taiwan School of Veterinary Medicine, investigators decided in 1986 to test the ability of acupuncture to treat pigs that had produced normal litters in the past but had stopped going into heat. The pigs were divided into three groups. The first group was treated with acupuncture. The second group received a relatively expensive treatment using hormones (prostaglandins). And the third group, which was designated a "control" group, received no treatment.

Of the pigs that received acupuncture, 83 percent went into heat immediately, and 92 percent of those had normal litters. Among those that were treated with prostaglandins, only 76 percent went into heat immediately, and 88 percent of them had normal litters. As for the control group, 50 percent eventually went into heat, and 75 percent of them had normal litters.

These and similar studies show clearly that acupuncture has a powerful potential to treat or cure a wide variety of animal health problems. These studies also demonstrate that acupuncture is not merely a placebo, since it works on animals (which do not have a concept of the placebo effect). I have discovered there is a remarkable range of health conditions that can be alleviated by acupuncture—and there are also a number of practical ways you can apply acupuncture principles at home, one-on-one with your pet.

CHAPTER NINE

How Acupuncture Can Work Wonders for Your Pet

The good doctor simply awakens the physician within.

—ALBERT SCHWEITZER

As a young vet starting out in practice, I wanted nothing more than to see every animal I treated leave the office healthy and happy. But no matter how hard I tried to find effective healing methods, there were always limits to what medicine and surgery could offer.

Then I discovered acupuncture. Today, when I step back from my practice, I'm still amazed at the range of possibilities for healing that acupuncture can offer an ailing animal. The complaint may be arthritis, paralysis, diarrhea, allergies, constipation, Lyme disease, mange, diabetes, a slipped disk, Wobbler's syndrome, deafness, or a host of other aches or pains. Regardless of the source of the problem, the chances are that acupuncture can at least help—and sometimes may be the key to a total cure. Acupuncture is not a panacea or "magic bullet," but it is an excellent way to help the body heal itself.

Furthermore, there seems to be no limit to the type of animal that can benefit from this procedure. Dogs, cats, horses, rabbits, pigs, birds, bulls, camels, llamas—they have all responded well to the stimulation of one acupoint or another.

To give you a more specific idea of exactly how your pet might benefit from acupuncture, I have delved into my own experience in treating many different types of patients. The

following "snapshots" from my practice will provide a view of
the inscrutable art of the needle.

HEALING A DOG WITH LYME DISEASE

Rocky had seemed hopeless. The black Labrador retriever had
once been a champion field trial dog. But then he contracted
Lyme disease, which had localized as a painful sweling in his
shoulder. As a result, he was lame and suffered from chronic
inflammation of the joints.

Another veterinarian had put him on antibiotics, and with
each pill, Rocky seemed to improve. But as soon as the drugs
were discontinued, his condition would decline again. With
nothing else to offer, the veterinarian, an orthopedist, had referred him to me for acupuncture.

From my vantage point, Rocky was far from over the hill. He
was still young—only about four years old. And despite the
soreness in his shoulder, the rest of his body seemed strong
and sturdy. I attacked his problem by inserting needles in localized points around the shoulder to relieve the inflammation.
In addition, I inserted needles in several points throughout his
body to build up the immune system and try to prevent the
Lyme disease from recurring. To give an added boost to
the treatment, I attached electrodes to the needles around
the shoulder in a procedure known as electroacupuncture.

Over the next six weeks, I gave Rocky weekly electroacupuncture treatments. By the third treatment, he was walking
with barely a trace of lameness; by the sixth treatment, he was
100 percent normal. Over the next year, he came back for
preventive "tune-ups" every three months, but neither his
lameness nor his Lyme disease ever reappeared.

Rocky's comeback was so complete that soon he was com-
peting in field trials again. In fact, he performed so well that
his owner was even offered $10,000 for him. This, for a dog
who not long before had been considered chronically lame!

As in Rocky's case, I've found that in treating Lyme, acupuncture often works quite well with antibiotics in a kind of double attack on the disease. In a paper I published in September 1991 I noted that researchers have found that the Lyme disease microorganism carried by deer ticks secretes what's called a "monocyte suppression factor"—a chemical that suppresses the immune system. The antibiotic works to kill the microorganism, and at the same time the acupuncture helps build up the immune system so that the animal's body can fight off the effects of the disease.

USING ACUPUNCTURE FOR ARTHRITIS

You've seen them—dogs that are so crippled from arthritis that they can barely stand on their hind legs. That was Pancho, a twelve-year-old German shepherd that had to be brought to me on a stretcher. His x-rays revealed that his hip sockets were so shallow they were practically nonexistent. He also had severe arthritis in his hips—a common ailment for certain large, older breeds, such as shepherds and Labrador retrievers. Every possible treatment had been tried on him using conventional medical techniques, but nothing seemed to alleviate his pain. Surgery was not appropriate due to his age as well as the heart and lung problems he had developed from a previous heartworm infection.

So, I applied electroacupuncture twice a week to Pancho's hips, back, and upper rear legs. Because he was getting on in years, I inserted needles in other locations on his legs which are sometimes known as "longevity points," acupoints that are associated with increased circulation throughout the body and may play a role in extending an animal's life span.

After four treatments, Pancho was able to stand on his own. With a few more sessions, he could move around more easily than had been possible in years. What's more, his owners and I could literally see the life flowing back into his whole body.

There was a gleam in his eye, his coat of light gray hair had a healthy sheen, and there was an improvement in his muscle tone.

Pancho went on to live to the ripe old age of seventeen—a senior citizenship he would never have reached if his arthritis had continued to plague him.

In a similar scenario, Joy, an eleven-year-old boxer, was unable to put weight on her left hind leg when I first saw her. She had been treated by a top orthopedic surgeon, who had used all sorts of arthritis medications to reduce the inflammation. These treatments had worked for a while, but then Joy lapsed back into a limp and gradually became so lame she couldn't put her leg down at all. Her x-rays showed that she had severe arthritis throughout her back and knees and neither drugs nor surgery could help.

At our first session together, I applied acupuncture to her back, upper left leg, and left knee. Within minutes, I could see that the needles were beginning to work their magic. Her little white face, which was punctuated by a patch of black over one eye, relaxed as the pain diminished with the release of endorphins into her system. Before long, she was fast asleep.

After eight treatments, she was finally able to put weight on her leg, and soon afterward she began to act like a normal dog. In fact, the last time I saw Joy she was jumping around play-fully, trying to catch a Frisbee!

HELPING A HORSE WITH COLIC

A few years ago, I was called out to a barn where a horse was suffering from ongoing gastrointestinal upsets, or "colic." Horses don't vomit—they just endure agonizing gas and pain in their intestinal tract, due to a variety of causes, such as parasites, impactions, or eating too much green grass. In this case, the poor horse, a twelve-year-old chestnut mare named Espresso, had been sick intermittently for more than a year.

Every four or five weeks, Espresso would have an attack of

colic. She would strike at the ground with her hoof in discomfort, and when the pain became unbearable, she would lie down and roll over to try to get relief. Each time, the veterinarian had to come out to the barn and give her a drug to ease the pain.

Obviously, nothing had worked for long, and after months of medicating the horse the owner was desperate for a more natural approach. I began treatment by carefully palpating the horse's back to check various acupuncture points for sensitivity. Only one was excruciatingly painful: Bladder 21—a point on the back at the end of the last rib, which is associated with stomach problems.

The best treatment seemed to me to be not regular use of a needle, which would have required a series of weekly visits, but rather acupressure massage—a technique that the owner could easily perform herself. This do-it-yourself approach would not only save money, but would also enhance the bonding between the woman and her horse.

After giving Espresso one acupuncture treatment on the sensitive point, I showed the owner how to massage the acupoint using a firm, counterclockwise movement with the tips of her index and middle fingers. With acupressure, it's been found that a counterclockwise motion tends to relax the patient, while a clockwise motion stimulates.

As I coached her along, the woman moved her fingers very slowly in a full circle and pressed down hard on the acupoint —a depression about the size of a quarter, located a hand's width from the midline of the horse's back. I explained to her how important it was to be sensitive to an animal's responses. If Espresso became irritable, she would know she was massaging too hard or too fast. If Espresso relaxed or fell asleep, the woman would know she had hit on just the right technique.

My prescription was that she perform a steady massage for five minutes at a time, once a day, over the acupoint. After the first few days of this treatment, Espresso became calmer and experienced fewer stomach upsets. Within about a week, the owner reported to me that a swelling, hot to the touch, had started at the spot where she was rubbing.

Then, incredibly, an abscess appeared at the site and burst. There may have been a chronic abscess deep inside the muscle that was impinging on a nerve. When the nerve was stimulated, it sent an impulse to the stomach, causing the spasm. Through the acupressure massage, the infection had come to the surface.

After the owner cleaned up the sore with a disinfectant, it healed over almost immediately. Even more remarkably, Espresso never suffered from colic again—and that was more than five years ago.

CURING AN ALLERGIC SIAMESE CAT

Mystery was a twelve-year-old Siamese crossbreed that had licked all the hair off her belly as a result of irritation from allergies. Ironically, this cat was allergic to most things that cats love—such as fish and milk, along with rugs, dust, and pollen.

One veterinarian had put Mystery on cortisone, but she began to develop side effects from the drug, such as excessive thirst, excessive urination, and certain behavioral changes. Then, to balance her hormones, Mystery was switched to a birth control pill for dogs, Ovaban, that is commonly used for this condition. The hormone worked for a while, but eventually the drug caused diabetes in the cat. A second veterinarian, a dermatologist, finally resolved the diabetes by taking her off Ovaban. His attempts at desensitization for the allergies worked for a while but proved futile in the long run. That was when he referred her to me.

When I first met Mystery, she licked her stomach nonstop. Even when I petted her, she licked and licked some more. She seemed obsessed, almost frantic to rid herself of this terrible itch. Not only was her stomach completely bare, but the rest of her coat was a dull, dry, grayish color, instead of its normal black.

As Mystery's owners held on to her lovingly, I stimulated

various acupuncture points on her body to balance her immune system and to counteract the allergic reactions. Six treatments later, Mystery looked as if she was wearing a ranch mink coat. Black, silky fur covered her whole body, and instead of licking incessantly, she lay calmly on the examining table in an elegant posture of repose. Her allergic reactions had disappeared.

As a result, I was able to taper off the acupuncture to once a month, then to every other month, and then, after a year, we suspended treatment completely. Four years later, when Mystery was seventeen, she began to scratch again—mainly because the owner had become lax in keeping her away from allergenic foods and other triggers. Acupuncture was able once again to bring her problems under control, and the last time I heard about her she was nineteen and still allergy-free.

RELIEVING A LLAMA'S STIFF NECK

Can you picture a llama with such severe arthritis in her neck that she couldn't move her head up or down? That's what greeted me one afternoon when a trailer pulled up to Brook Farm Veterinary Center, where I see my patients. Out of the trailer came a llama, whose neck, usually supple as a swan's, was literally stiff as a board. It jutted out from her body at a 45-degree angle and couldn't be moved more than a few inches. In order to eat, the animal had to nibble grains from a bowl on a high stool stacked with phone books.

The llama was an elderly creature under the care of Dawn Animal Agency, a kind of nursing home for abandoned zoo animals and also a source of animal talent for Radio City Music Hall and other theatrical productions. Luckily for the llama, her owners approached her treatment with missionary zeal. That was why they were willing to load her up in a trailer and drive more than an hour to my clinic for acupuncture.

I inserted needles behind the llama's ear, in front of her shoulder blades, and in the spaces between the vertebrae in her neck. As soon as I put in the needles, the muscles became so relaxed that her whole neck drooped before our eyes. Then she lay down on the ground with her legs tucked under her and let her head hang limply as she rested.

For the first time in a year, the llama was free of stiffness. A week later, she came back for a second treatment, and from then on she was able to hold her head up and move it around with ease. Now, more than two years later, only cold, damp weather causes the neck to begin to get stiff again.

ELIMINATING EPILEPSY IN AN ALASKAN MALAMUTE

A ten-year-old Alaskan malamute, a beautiful gray-and-white sled dog, had been racked for more than a year by twelve to fourteen epileptic seizures a month. He had been to a veterinary neurologist and placed on phenobarbital, but the medicine failed to stop the seizures. In fact, the drug caused the malamute to be constantly depressed.

When I first saw him, the dog appeared to be in a daze. His eyes had a glassy stare, and from his body language I could see that he was so beaten down that the term "hangdog" would have been a charitable description.

Under general anesthesia, I inserted a set of 24-karat gold implants into acupoints along the muscles on the midline of the dog's skull and also on a lateral line between the midline and the ears. With this procedure, it's necessary to thread fine jewelers' wire through the acupoints with a needle. The gold wire has the effect of stimulating the acupoints over the long term.

Almost immediately, the seizures stopped. Gradually, I was able to taper off the phenobarbital to a much lower level, and before long the dog was happy and alert. He lived happily for three more years, then died from unrelated causes.

In a similar case, I treated a seven-year-old Airedale terrier named Curly that had epileptic seizures a couple of times a week. Such problems can be hereditary, or they can come on suddenly as a result of trauma. In Curly's case, I decided a special metal ear tack might work in one acupoint just inside the ear. A colleague of mine, John Van Niekert at the University of South Africa, had reported an 80 percent success rate controlling seizures with such a procedure.

So, following his example, I placed a tack in Curly's ear. The "ornament" was affixed in a secure fashion with tape and Superglue. Then the dog trotted out with his owner, and I didn't hear from them for two years, when the owner made another appointment.

"Since you put in the ear tack, Curly never had another seizure—until now," the owner said.

The minute I saw Curly, I knew why his seizures had returned. The ear tack had fallen out! So I put in another one, and once again the seizures stopped.

INDUCING LABOR IN A CAT

The four-year-old Burmese cat was already in labor when her owner, a breeder, rushed her to my clinic. The cat had a history of problems giving birth, and this time the owner didn't want to take any chances. In a previous pregnancy, the cat had delivered one kitten, and subsequent pregnancies had resulted in a series of stillborn births.

"From the x-rays and physical exam she looks like she needs a C-section," I said, as I watched her straining to push the kittens out.

My partner at the time, Dr. Evan Kanouse, agreed. "This is definitely a cesarean. I'll scrub up," he said.

But then I had another thought. "Let me try some acupuncture first."

"Okay, while I'm prepping for surgery, you try the acupuncture," he replied.

Talk about pressure. But I immediately began electroacupuncture by sending electrical impulses into some key acupoints in an effort to stimulate uterine contractions and dilation of the cervix. Within four or five minutes, the cat started having contractions, and three tiny kittens popped out—boom, boom, boom—right in front of our eyes.

The owner was ecstatic, the technician and I were cheering, and my partner's mouth dropped open. Of course, he had to take off his surgical gloves.

This technique has also worked well with dogs, and I have every reason to think that many animals that have had difficulty in labor might benefit.

RAISING A STUD BULL'S SPERM COUNT

One of the top breeding bulls in all of North America started to have problems with infertility. His sperm had been among the most potent, best-producing in the history of a New York firm that specialized in artificial insemination for milk cows. This bull's offspring produced some of the best milk the dairy industry had ever seen—and so when he began to run into sexual difficulties, his owners became understandably upset.

It seemed that the bull had developed arthritis of the spine as a result of the constant mounting and ejaculation he had been required to perform. The breeders routinely brought in a "teaser" cow to get him excited, and then he would hop up onto an artificial humping device, where he would ejaculate and have his sperm collected.

But then, during a short period of time, his sperm count declined from the richest in the land to nearly zero. A top neurologist and also a reproduction expert at a university veterinary school determined that he had developed arthritis of the spine, which impinged on certain nerve roots that were instrumental in his sperm production. I noticed from pictures taken of him that he had severe muscle atrophy on his right side—apparently a direct result of the arthritis.

His condition was so serious and the prognosis so dismal that his owners were ready to get rid of him. But then one of the university veterinarians suggested that acupuncture might

be of some benefit. As it happened, a colleague trained in acupuncture consulted with me over the telephone and then began
treatment.

I told him to use electroacupuncture to stimulate the governing vessel and the bladder meridian, which lay over the nerves
that were being affected. The vet proceeded to give the bull six
treatments. After this initial series of sessions, the bull's sperm
count not only went back up to normal, it actually rose to a
higher level than ever before!

Now a skeptic might say, "Well, probably with a little rest
that bull's sperm count would have gone back up anyway." But
the problem with that argument is that when the vets tried
easing off the acupuncture, the sperm count went back down
again. It became clear that the bull's improvement was directly
related to the acupuncture.

What the acupuncture was doing in this case was relieving
the arthritic inflammation in the bull's body and also stimulating the damaged nerves. The veterinarian who continued to
perform the hands-on treatment finally implanted gold in the
acupoints and got the higher sperm counts to last for eight
weeks before another electroacupuncture session was required. The veterinarian currently flies up every two months
to treat this bull with acupuncture—a practice he has been
following now for five years.

Acupuncture won't always work on an ailing pet. But the clinical results and research support for this procedure with many
diseases are so unambiguous you should definitely consider
acupuncture as an alternative—if all other attempts at treatment have failed.

Although you should always consult a veterinary acupuncture expert to deal with serious illness, there are some simple
acupressure techniques every pet owner can apply to help the
healing process along. Knowledge of six critical acupoints will
help you relieve temporary distress and give first aid to your
pet in a crisis. Two of these points are emergency points, while
the other four are called "master points," acupoints that are

known to have generalized beneficial effects on the body and can also help in particular types of diseases.

SIX ESSENTIAL ACUPOINTS— AND HOW YOU CAN USE THEM ON YOUR PET

Before you attempt to apply acupressure yourself, keep in mind a few basic principles. First, use the tip of your index or middle finger or your thumb to apply pressure to the chosen acupoint. You should press firmly but gently. If your cat, dog, or horse flinches or cries out, you're probably pressing too hard.

Second, if you want to relax your animal, rub in a circular motion counterclockwise over the acupoint. If you want to stimulate him, rub clockwise.

Finally, in the following descriptions of acupoint locations, I'll be using human terminology such as "knee," "elbow," "hand," and "foot." To translate this language to your animal's anatomy, just imagine he is standing on his hind legs like a human. The precise location of these points on a dog, which are similar to those in many other animals, can be found on the drawing on page 148.

Acupoint #1: Emergency Point for Cardiac Arrest

As I mentioned earlier, if you and your pet were stranded on a deserted island where there were no veterinary facilities, one of the acupoints I would want you to know is "Governing Vessel 26," or GV26 (see drawing on page 147). If you know where GV26 is located—centered just below the nose and above the upper lip—you'll be in a position to hasten the recovery of a pet that has gone into cardiac arrest or a state of shock. A series of sharp jabs at this acupoint with your fingernail or with a needle will stimulate the body's production of the fight-or-flight hormone, adrenaline (also called epinephrine), and the chances will improve that the animal revives. A word of warning: You should never stimulate this point on a conscious ani-

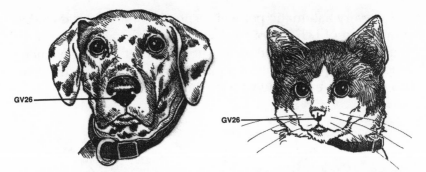

Acupunture Points for Cardiac and Respiratory Suppression in the Dog and Cat (GV26)

mal or you risk getting a nasty bite. You may, however, use it on newborn pups that are having difficulty breathing.

Acupoint #2: Emergency Point for Asthmatic Attacks

Another critical emergency point, especially for asthmatic cats, is what the Chinese call "Lung 7," or LU7, which is located on the inside of the front paw, just above the wrist bone. One of my patients, a seven-year-old white Persian, had developed asthma and suffered from periodic bouts of uncontrollable wheezing despite appropriate medications. After three acupuncture treatments in my office, she had improved dramatically, but her owner was concerned about how to handle acute attacks in the middle of the night. I showed him how to massage the cat's front paws at LU7, which can alleviate a variety of respiratory problems.

My demonstration came none too soon. A few nights later, the cat started panting, wheezing, and gasping for breath. Without wasting a moment, her owner massaged LU7, and within seconds the cat began to breathe more easily. Eventually, she calmed down and slept peacefully through the night. With his very own hands, the cat's owner had been able to reverse a potentially life-threatening situation. In the past, he said, such wheezing had always turned into full-blown asthmatic attacks.

Not every asthmatic pet will respond as this one did to the stimulation of LU7. If your cat is having an attack, it's critical to administer prescribed medications and get him to an emergency room quickly. But in a pinch, having an alternative like LU7 might save you and your pet hours of anguish.

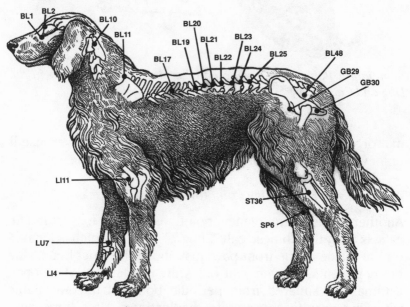

Acupunture Points in the Dog

Each acupuncture point has many uses on its own and in combination with others. Here are a few simple applications of the illustrated points, clockwise from bottom left.

LI4	(Large Intestine 4). Front leg problems; head, sinus, and neck problems.
LU7	(Lung 7). Respiratory problems.
LI11	(Large Intestine 11). Local elbow problems.
BL1–2	(Bladder 1–2). Calming points.
BL10–11	(Bladder 10–11). Local neck problems.
BL17, BL19–25,	(Bladder 17, 19–25). Local back problems.
BL48, GB29–30	(Bladder 48, Gall Bladder 29–30). Hip problems.
ST36	(Stomach 36). Local knee problems; digestive upset.
SP6	(Spleen 6). Hormonal problems.

Along with such emergency points as GV26 and LU7, there are four critical master points that, when stimulated, are beneficial for the overall well-being of your pet.

Acupoint #3: Master Point for an Upset Stomach or Other Gastrointestinal Complaints

Exerting pressure at a point known as "Stomach 36," or ST36, with the fingertips can help relieve gastrointestinal problems. This is such a valuable point that the Chinese have a special name for it—"Walk Three Miles"—presumably because of the increased energy one receives once the point is stimulated. This point is located just below the knee on the outside of the shinbone, in a depression where muscles of the lower leg join the knee.

Whenever I think of ST36, I'm reminded of a three-year-old bull mastiff named Sarge that had a history of digestive problems and diarrhea and had been diagnosed with inflammatory bowel disease. I was treating Sarge with acupuncture, along with a bland diet of fish and potatoes, or lamb and rice, and his condition had turned around. But his owner wanted to know some acupressure techniques she could use if the condition recurred when she was at her mountain house, far from any vet. I taught her how to apply acupressure to Stomach 36.

A few months later, Sarge discovered a bag of chocolate chip cookies and promptly consumed them. He ended up lying on his side, belching and squirming from gas pains. Seeing his distress, his owner massaged ST36 in a counterclockwise direction for five minutes on each hind leg. Within a few minutes, the grumbling in his stomach quieted down, and Sarge relaxed and went to sleep. By the next morning, he was fully recovered.

It's important to note, however, that the syndrome that afflicted Sarge should not be confused with bloat, which has similar symptoms, including belching, pain, and a swollen stomach. Bloat is indeed a medical emergency and should be handled immediately by a veterinarian.

Acupoint #4: Master Point for Head and Neck Aches

The acupoint known as "Large Intestine 4," or LI4, is located on the hand, or front paw, near the point where the thumb and index finger meet. It's one of the important "longevity" points that increase microcirculation and can contribute to a longer, healthier life. Using acupressure here with your pet may soothe neck aches, pains in the front leg and shoulder, nasal conges- tion, and even diarrhea or constipation. Stimulating this point is also good for relieving headaches in people.

Another word of warning: Many dogs and cats don't like to have their paws touched. So be sure to approach this acupoint gingerly. And don't massage it at all if your dog or cat becomes aggressive when his toes are touched.

Even though an animal may suffer from head or neck dis- tress, it's unlikely he will be able to indicate to you directly what's wrong. So be sure to have a proper diagnosis by a veterinarian and then sensitize yourself to recognize subtle signals. To locate your pet's pain, you can watch his body language to see if his back is hunched up, for example, or whether he is holding his neck unusually low.

Master point LI4 came in handy for a nine-year-old pug that I was treating for a stiff neck. During regular acupuncture treat- ments, the dog relaxed the minute I inserted a needle into LI4. But one weekend, in between treatments, he slid down a cou- ple of steps and jolted his neck, causing a relapse of the stiff- ness.

His alert owner remembered the pug's contentment when I did acupuncture on LI4. Without any prompting from me, he massaged the point on the front paw, and the dog's muscles relaxed markedly.

You might also consider massaging LI4 if your pet has a congested nose. The nostrils are at the end of an acupuncture meridian that begins near LI4. In other words, you can actually help clear his nostrils by massaging an acupoint that's relatively far away!

Acupoint #5: Master Point for the Immune System, Allergies, and Metabolic Imbalances

This acupoint, called "Large Intestine 11," or LI11, is located on the outside of the elbow joint, where the biceps join the forearm. In Chinese medicine, this point is known as *qu chi,* or Pond-in-the-Curve, because it is in a depression at the curve in the elbow. Applying acupressure here can reduce pain in the shoulder and elbow.

Massaging this point can be the key to alleviating arthritis discomfort, as it was for a Bernese mountain dog I was treating. The dog had suffered from severe arthritis in his elbows and had improved so much through acupuncture that he was back running and playing again. But during one backyard outing, he twisted his elbow and had a spasm. His owner massaged LI11, the spasm subsided immediately, and the dog was back playing again.

In another case, a shaggy Tibetan terrier I was treating for arthritis in the elbows started limping during a three-month hiatus in office visits. A simple five-minute massage in a counterclockwise direction by her owner cleared up the limp on the spot.

Acupoint #6: Master Point for Endocrine Disorders

Spleen 6, or SP6, can work wonders for menstrual cramps in humans. In animals, stimulating this point, located on the inside of the foot on the rear legs just to the front and above the heel, can help a variety of endocrine problems, including diabetes.

Not long ago, I was giving acupuncture to a cat with arthritis when his owner happened to mention in passing that the cat also had diabetes. What's more, she said, his insulin was especially difficult to regulate.

"Why not try acupuncture?" I suggested.

Immediately, using Spleen 6, I began acupuncture on the cat. I also showed the owner how to massage the point in between visits.

She dutifully massaged the acupoint every day for five minutes in a counterclockwise direction. At the next visit, she couldn't contain her excitement. For the first time in a year, the cat's blood sugar and insulin levels were approaching normal.

It's impossible to say, of course, how much of this cat's improvement was due to the acupressure and how much was due to acupuncture. I do know that, in general, there is no substitute for the needle; it goes deeper and provides a stronger stimulation to the acupoint. But I will never dispute the potent healing possibilities in the application of acupressure—along with the bond of friendship that is strengthened in those moments of contact between a pet and a human.

Of course, your animal doesn't have to be sick for you to apply acupressure techniques. There are also a number of ways to use acupressure to massage your healthy cat, dog, or horse. The idea is to rub key acupoints in order to produce relaxation, increase circulation, enhance human-to-animal bonding, and in general promote the overall well-being of your pet.

Massage of Your Dog's Back for General Well-Being

THE SECRETS OF ANIMAL MASSAGE

The techniques of effective massage are similar to the kind of acupressure that works best for specific medical therapy or first aid on your pet. But when you're trying to relax a healthy pet, there are a few additional variations. The basic principles are:

- Apply steady, rotating pressure with a fingertip to a particular acupoint on the animal. If you want to relax your pet, rub counterclockwise. If you want to stimulate him, rub clockwise.
- Breathe deeply, regularly, and slowly as you massage—a practice that will help you maintain a steady rhythm in your rubbing.
- Give your pet a complete massage at least once a day for the best results.
- As part of a massage program, encourage your pet to stretch different parts of his body to promote the sense of well-being that accompanies greater flexibility.

In general, I would suggest that you *avoid* massage or any other acupressure method if the following conditions are present:

- Your pet has just eaten. You should wait at least two hours before you try any acupressure.
- Your pet is sick. Generally speaking, neither animals nor humans like to be touched if they are wrestling with bodily pain, an infection, a fever, or a disease.
- Your pet is pregnant. You could possibly induce premature labor.
- Your pet has just been exercising intensely. Allow the heart rate to come down and the panting to stop before you try any acupressure.

Below are some ways that a complete home massage program can make three different types of pets—dogs, cats, and horses—feel not just good but *great*. If you happen to have another kind of animal that responds well to caressing or touching, any of these massage techniques should work well because acupuncture is based on scientific principles that cut across species lines.

SMALL ANIMAL MASSAGE

A Siamese cat who was suffering from a ruptured ligament in the knee joint was brought to my office for treatment, and I could see immediately that the knee joint was arthritic. A previous vet had tried putting the leg in a cast, but that hadn't worked. Then an orthopedist had operated on the leg and managed to stabilize the knee, but the cat still wouldn't put any weight on it. So the orthopedist recommended that the owner come to me for acupuncture.

It was obvious that the owner thought that acupuncture was a lot of hocus-pocus, and he as much as told me so. I immediately decided that it would be best to get all our feelings out in the open.

"I sense that you really don't believe in this acupuncture procedure," I said. "You're probably saying to yourself, 'I don't believe I'm here, doing this.' "

"Yes, I *am* saying that," the owner said. "That's exactly how I feel."

"I don't blame you," I replied. "It's natural to think that sticking needles in an animal is weird. I used to feel that way myself—until I learned how this approach can produce healing where other methods fail."

Despite his doubts, the owner decided to go ahead with the treatment. So I placed needles in the cat's knee and all up and down the leg, tracing the line of the sciatic nerve. Then I showed him how to massage the animal's leg.

"Massage is an essential part of this treatment," I told him. "The acupuncture will work much better if you combine it with specific pressure on the acupoints along with a generalized massage program between our sessions."

In fact, after only six acupuncture sessions—with massage applied between each session—the owner came into my office and announced, "My cat isn't lame anymore!"

He's now a complete believer in acupuncture *and* he massages his pet practically every day.

Here's an outline of the home massage program that worked for his cat—and may work for your dog or cat as well.

The most effective massage technique involves first doing a general massage. Then, once your pet is relaxed, you can focus on the injured part of the pet's body. Of course, if your pet isn't injured, you can skip the therapeutic massage.

General Body Massage

Along with the specific therapeutic massage for the injured knee, I recommended a more general body massage to help energize the pet—a technique I would suggest that you use with your cat or dog daily, regardless of whether or not he's sick or injured. But if your pet resists at all, do not proceed. First stretch out each of the animal's legs. Then massage, using the following technique:

• For both front legs, press the depression on the triceps toward the back of the shoulder on the acupoint known as Small Intestine 9, or SI9, illustrated on page 156. Then for at least thirty seconds, rotate your index finger in a counterclockwise direction to relax your pet, or a clockwise direction to stimulate him.

• Next, still concentrating on the front legs, move down to LI4, the depression where the animal's "thumb" and "forefinger" meet, and press gently with your forefinger. Activating this spot may have beneficial effects in the neck, head, shoulder, and front legs. This pressure can be performed on each foot.

• Now, beginning at the base of the pet's neck, move down the "bladder meridian," which is traced just to each side of the spine along the long muscles that stretch from the neck to the lower back. Use the tip of your finger to find depressions in and between the muscles, and press gently for about thirty seconds on each spot. Another technique is to use both your forefinger and thumb so that you can massage the muscles on each side of the spine simultaneously. A counterclockwise movement during this part of the massage will relax a stiff back and adjoining muscles.

• Next, begin to massage the muscle depressions around the hips with your fingertips. Use the familiar rotating movement for at least thirty seconds in each depression you find. This technique may provide benefits for the hip and hindquarter region of the cat or dog. (I'm reminded of a fifteen-year-old Labrador that was brought in to me because of arthritis in the hip. I performed acupuncture in the hip region, specifically in "Gallbladder 30"—depicted in the illustration below—and surrounding acupoints. Then I directed the owner to massage the hip area, in this case using a clockwise motion because of a

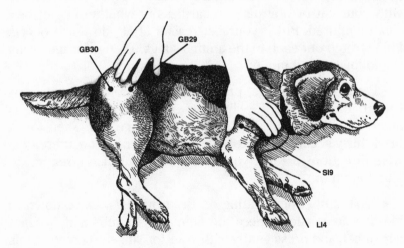

Acupressure Points for Arthritis in the Hips (GB29 and 30), Stiffness in the Front Legs (SI9), and Beneficial Effects in the Neck, Head, Shoulder, and Front Legs (LI4)

need to strengthen and stimulate the dog. The massage helped strengthen the animal and enabled him to walk more easily for more than a year—until he finally died at the ripe old age of sixteen.)

• If you want to help your pet relax completely, finish off your massage with a slow, gentle rubbing of each ear and the top of the skull. This kind of contact induces great peace and calm in the animal—almost guaranteed to produce contented sighs in your dog and exquisite purrs in your feline.

Using this general massage program on your cat or dog every day—along with specific, therapeutic acupressure if he has some ailment—can greatly improve the animal's health. Just keep in mind that if the pet tends to be lethargic or weak, clockwise movement will perk him up. If he is nervous or "hyper," counterclockwise movement will calm him down.

Therapeutic Massage

The cat owner stretched out the injured leg to prepare the muscles for massage. With the animal lying on its side, the owner grasped the back leg, just above the injured knee, and gently pulled downward, outward and inward, backward and forward on the muscles. Then he held the foot and ankle area firmly and once more pulled *gently* downward, so that the muscles were stretched out. Gentleness was particularly important in this case because of the cat's damaged knee.

"Watch the animal's reaction," I had told him. If there was no wincing or other pain-related response, he was probably applying just the right amount of downward pressure.

After about thirty seconds of this stretching, the owner began to massage each of the acupoints on the cat's knee and along the leg, where the needles had been placed during the sessions in the clinic. The acupoints tend to be located in depressions and valleys in between the muscles.

Generally speaking, acupoints in a cat are rather small, about the circumference of a wide pen point. As a result, massage can be most effectively applied with a single fingertip. With a dog, they tend to vary in size from a pen point to an eraser end. For larger dogs, you might want to use two fingers to do the massage.

In this particular case, I told the cat owner to use the clockwise motion as he rubbed the acupoints with his index finger. This way, he would be more likely to stimulate and strengthen the leg muscles.

LARGE ANIMAL MASSAGE

A client of mine had an elderly mare that developed a sore back. I began to do some acupuncture on her, and following each treatment she drifted off to sleep. After two of these sessions, the horse got noticeably better, and so I decided to switch our approach to massage by the owner.

The owner focused on two acupoints, known as "Bladder 25," at the end of the back, on either side of the spine just at the top of the haunches. Please note that in a dog, these points are closer to the middle of the back. In a horse, the acupoints are much larger than in a smaller animal; they may reach the size of a quarter. Feeling the depression between the muscles at these points, the owner massaged counterclockwise to relax the animal. Then she performed a more general massage down the horse's spine, on the neck, and on the ears, which helped to further relieve the sore back.

Before embarking on any home treatment, consult with your veterinarian to make sure there are no medical reasons why your horse would not be a good candidate for therapeutic acupressure. Then try these general massage techniques prior to riding. Because of the relatively large size of a horse's acupoints, you can use the tips of more than one finger, a knuckle, or even a fist.

• To relax your animal's hindquarters, as I just described in the story of the mare with the sore back, focus on Bladder 25.

You should massage counterclockwise for two to three minutes at the acupoints on both the right and left sides.

• To further relax the haunches and muscles leading to the tail, try some tail pulls and releases. All you have to do is grab the tail about ten to twelve inches from the root and stretch gently back and down, and then up. You should also rotate the tail in a counterclockwise motion to induce relaxation.

Some suggest that these movements must be performed while you're standing close, squarely behind the horse, and certainly, that makes it easy to manipulate the tail. If your horse isn't a kicker, this stance may be just fine. But if you have any fear that you may get kicked, stand off to the side.

• For upper-body relaxation, massage the center of the horse's head just above the eyes. Move your fingertips slowly and gently in a counterclockwise direction over the "whorl" of hair.

• In order to induce overall relaxation and calm, if your horse is not head-shy, finish off the session by gently massaging each of the horse's ears, beginning at the center of the ear and moving up to the tip. The ear contains a number of important acupuncture points that can produce a general sense of well-being.

In addition to massage, it's also important to get your horse involved in regular flexibility exercises. Just massaging his neck won't do the job, but by using a technique I call "carrot-practic," which involves the use of a long carrot to entice the horse to move, you can enhance his ability to relax. But first a word of caution: Make sure that you use a *long* carrot or strands of hay. If you use something that's too short, the horse may nip your fingers.

Flexibility Exercise #1

Stand on the horse's right side near the rump, with your front facing toward the animal. Hold a carrot in your right hand and grasp the horse's tail with your left. Then encourage the horse to reach around by bending his neck toward you to get the carrot. Keep holding the tail so that the animal won't be able to turn around and face you to get the carrot. You want the horse to curve and stretch his neck.

Occasionally, you'll hear popping sounds as the horse flexes his neck, and that's just fine; you want to encourage some adjustments of the neck and spine. If the horse can't flex his head completely around, that may indicate he has a stiff neck or some vertebral misalignments. In such a case, acupuncture or chiropractic by a professionally trained veterinarian may be beneficial.

Now, execute the same neck-stretching exercise on the left side of the horse. I recommend doing these movements once or twice both before and after riding.

Flexibility Exercise #2

This time, place the carrot between the horse's front legs by his knees, so that he has to stretch down, as though he's executing a bow. This will enhance flexibility in the neck from another direction.

Massage, stretching, acupuncture, and therapeutic acupressure have the capacity to work hand-in-glove with traditional veterinary medicine, or even to heal diseases or conditions that traditional techniques can't handle. And the regular physical contact that these programs require can do wonders to cement the bond between you and your pet.

But my journey of healing hasn't ended with acupuncture and its related disciplines. As I witnessed the animals under my care becoming transformed through the needle into pain-free, vibrant creatures, I felt myself moving to a new level of expectancy. Acupuncture had more than fulfilled its promise, and now I was ready to move on to experience new horizons of health.

CHAPTER TEN

The Potency of Nature's Own Prescriptions

Natural forces are the healers of disease.

—HIPPOCRATES

Because alternative health treatments have gained such wide acceptance these days, it's increasingly common to hear someone at an otherwise conservative gathering respond to a medical complaint with the question "Have you tried herbs?" In the Western medical and scientific community, on the other hand, such a suggestion about an herbal remedy can still conjure up images of shamans and witch doctors. But the general public is more open to the idea—and rightly so. Before the advent of modern medicine, folk practitioners *knew* that herbs really worked. Through a process of trial and error spanning centuries, they discovered that certain parts of plants could relieve headaches, colds, infections, insomnia, and a variety of other ills.

In the seventeenth century, for example, European explorers learned that the bark of the South American cinchona tree could be used to treat malaria. In fact, the cinchona remedy became so popular that the supply began to run out. In response to the shortage, the Englishman Edward Stone started to experiment in the late eighteenth century with bark from the willow tree, which he finally concluded could effectively lower fevers. The reason for this benefit became evident later when acetylsalicylic acid—which we know as aspirin—was identified as a component of the willow tree bark.

Similarly, herbalists found centuries ago that the purple coneflower, echinacea, could reduce inflammation and infections. And for those who were too tense to get a good night's sleep, the root of the valerian plant came to be used as a sedative and treatment for anxiety. In fact, countless herbal remedies have evolved over the centuries. In the materia medica compiled by the Greek pharmacologist Pedanius Dioscorides in A.D. 77, about one thousand plant-based remedies were listed.

I became a believer in the benefits of herbs for sick animals, and a practitioner in herbal medicine, only a few years ago. But the more I have used these traditional remedies, the more convinced I have become that the ancients had access to important knowledge that is essential for us to understand if we are to provide our pets with the highest possible levels of good health.

My initiation into the ways of the herb began when I met Ihor Basko, a Ukrainian-American who now lives in Hawaii and is a pioneer in the use of Chinese herbs with animals. While I was taking a course in Kentucky on animal acupuncture, I attended a lecture on herbs given by Ihor and immediately afterward I insisted that he have dinner with me. He regaled me with the virtues of herbal remedies, and I found myself calculating how to use this method of healing in my own practice.

The opportunity came when a sick cat, an altered Abyssinian, was brought into my office with a bladder and urinary tract infection. His coat was getting dull, and the antibiotics he had been prescribed seemed to be doing more harm than good. The owner expressed an interest in acupuncture, but I had another suggestion: "Let's try him on herbs first."

Initially, I designed an organic, high-fiber diet to build up the cat's immune system. Then I selected a basic Chinese herbal combination—a fungal concoction known as Polyporus—to treat the bladder infection. Traditional Chinese medicine typically involves combining several different herbs. One may be used to enhance the healing impact of a second; or a particular herb may be used to counter the side effects of another.

Doctors in our own culture tend to be more reductionistic in their prescriptions. They frequently pick just one drug to attack a particular disease or set of symptoms, and more often than not, unpleasant side effects will result. The Chinese may be less "scientific" in our sense of the word, but they are more synergistic, with a focus on how an array of herbs or other treatments will affect the *whole* person or animal.

Although I had been impressed by Ihor's lectures and the literature he directed me to, I didn't start to become really confident about herbal treatments until I saw that Abyssinian *cured* of his problem within a week! The sheen in his coat improved, his energy returned, and all signs of the infection disappeared.

In subsequent years, I have made use of scores of herbs to treat many different animals with a wide variety of illnesses and complaints. To describe them all would require an entire book in itself. But I do want to give you a taste of what herbal remedies can do for your pet, and to that end, I have compiled my own personal list of the top nine herbs you should know about. These important herbs are the ones I have used with the greatest frequency in dealing with specific diseases and conditions. I have found that they provide potent healing responses with the fewest side effects. But before I go into the details, let me mention a few caveats.

• First and foremost, you should *never* use herbs on your own to treat your pet. Herbs used by expert healers from the Chinese, Native American, and other cultures can be quite powerful. With an inadequate understanding of their power and side effects, you could do your pet much more harm than good. So before you use herbs, be sure that you have the guidance and close supervision of a qualified veterinarian who has had some advanced training in herbal medicine.

• Herbs are usually most effective when used on smaller animals, like cats and dogs. (Horses or other large animals tend to require herbs in such large quantities that the expense can be prohibitive. Also, consuming herbs in very large amounts can interfere with the animal's appetite and cause him to eat too little, depriving him of important nutrients.)

• Generally speaking, herbs should be used in combination —not alone.

MY PERSONAL TOP NINE HERBAL REMEDIES

Remedy #1: Yunnan Paiyao

This herbal formula, which is linked to Hunan Province in China, first came to the wide attention of Americans during the Vietnam War. The Viet Cong carried it in their first aid kits to stanch the blood flow from gunshot wounds. They would swallow a "hit pill" consisting of the formula and also pour a powdered form over the wound itself.

Although the exact formula is a closely guarded secret known only by the Chinese manufacturer in the province of Hunan, a critical ingredient is the herb tien chi ginseng, which promotes clotting of the blood. As a result, Yunnan Paiyao is not only one of the most potent blood-clotting agents in existence for treating traumatic injuries, but it has also been used in the Far East for centuries to fight skin infections, abscesses, sore throats, bleeding ulcers, and related problems. Ihor Basko was the first to introduce me to this formula and to report that it worked well with dogs and cats suffering from postsurgical bleeding.

My first recollection of actually using the remedy myself involved a five-year-old female collie that had been spayed while she was in heat. This procedure, which involves the removal of the ovaries and uterus, is usually done when the animal is not in heat to avoid the possibility of excessive internal bleeding. But the owners insisted on the spaying and, predictably, some bleeding occurred from small blood vessels after surgery.

I felt that the best approach in this case would be to try Yunnan Paiyao. First, as I always do before using herbs, I cautioned the owners that even though I'm convinced of the potential benefits of herbal remedies, they are still considered an unconventional and controversial procedure. But there wasn't much of a chance they would deny their permission since the dog was steadily growing weaker. So I gave the collie the herbal pill, and within fifteen minutes the bleeding stopped completely.

It was hard not to become a true believer after that. And the more I saw, the more convinced I became that Western medicine has been missing out on a huge area of veterinary healing. I have been particularly impressed by the way Yunnan Paiyao can help dogs that have suffered severe trauma. More than once, I have seen it perform miracles for an animal hit by a car—a tragic circumstance that always upsets me.

One day, I examined a husky that had been slammed and nearly killed by a speeding vehicle and was rushed to the animal hospital semiconscious and in a state of shock, with significant hemorrhaging into the abdomen. I could actually feel the fluid sloshing around when I pressed on the animal's abdomen. Relying on conventional techniques to treat shock, we gave the husky intravenous injections of corticosteroids and fluids to try to stabilize him. But this approach didn't work, and the internal bleeding continued.

My concern was growing by the second. "This is a dog we should operate on immediately," I said, convinced that surgical intervention was the way to go. But I had a real dilemma since it was also evident that if we did proceed with surgery at this point, the animal might not recover at all. The anesthesia we would have to administer would deepen the state of shock—and that, of course, could result in death.

So we were caught between a classic rock and a hard place. The only other option seemed to be herbs—specifically Yunnan Paiyao.

The dog was conscious enough to open his mouth and swallow. So I stuffed the herbal capsule deep into his throat and held his mouth together until he swallowed. I waited prayerfully, not knowing what would happen. But in a few minutes, the dog's condition stabilized, and shortly afterward he emerged from shock. Even more important, the herbs stopped the internal bleeding, and we didn't have to resort to surgery at all. We observed the dog cautiously through the night in the hospital and then sent him home happy and stable the next day.

Another dog, a border collie, was hit by a car and suffered a scrape down to the bone on a front leg. He was in shock, blood was pouring out of the wound, and the bone, which had been laid bare for several inches, was caked with dirt. We cleaned the wound and wrapped pressure bandages around the wound to halt the blood flow, but when we unwrapped them, the bleeding started again. The blood wasn't clotting because so many small vessels in the leg had been ruptured.

Finally, after about fifteen minutes of futile effort, I suggested that we try Yunnan Paiyao. We poured some of the formula over the scraped area and gave more to the dog orally. The blood began to clot within minutes, before our very eyes. The fluid seeped out of the wound, but then dark red clumps would form, and as the clotting occurred, the collie began to perk up. Within about twenty minutes, the bleeding stopped and we were able to begin suturing the wound.

Yunnan Paiyao is *not* intended to be a substitute for ligation, the tying off of a major vein or artery. But when many small vessels have been broken and ligating isn't possible, this herbal remedy can work like magic. It can also be useful for treating a wide spectrum of diseases that cause bleeding. A geriatric Doberman pinscher had a malignant melanoma in the mouth, but the animal was also suffering from Von Willebrand's disease, which involves a tendency to bleed easily. Such a combination of problems can make performing surgery a touchy affair. Part of the dog's jaw would have to be removed, and that would increase the risk of excessive bleeding to the point, perhaps, of death. But the tumor made it very uncomfortable for the Doberman to eat; his mouth would bleed and hurt every time he tried to chew. A decision had to be made.

After considering their options, the owners finally decided not to remove the tumor but to make every effort to keep their pet as comfortable as possible. Yunnan Paiyao was the way we achieved that. After seven days on this herbal regimen, the bleeding in his mouth stopped for about a month. When it started up again, I began to administer the herbs for a second course. We eventually discovered that giving the dog Yunnan

Paiyao about once a month for a few consecutive days would stop the bleeding completely.

As I gained experience with this herbal formula, I realized that it was best to use it on a short-term basis. Administering it daily or more frequently than a few times a month can cause side effects, such as liver problems. But used on a restricted basis, Yunnan Paiyao brings good results with no adverse effects for most animals.

I have also used this potent remedy to fight skin infections. One German shepherd had a bacterial skin infection, with little round pustules covering his back and abdomen, and when they burst, they became red, raw, ugly circles, about an inch in diameter. The dog scratched them constantly and, of course, that made matters worse.

Normally, this condition is treated with antibiotics, but the bacteria in this particular case were resistant to everything we tried. We tested four different antibiotics, and after a while none of them worked anymore. Then we turned to iodine baths. Again, this helped for a time, and then the infections returned. We put the dog on a complete vegetarian diet. Still, no long-term improvement. Finally, I decided to try Yunnan Paiyao—one capsule, twice a day. After three days the condition began to clear up, and by the end of one week the sores had healed and the infection had disappeared.

Although Yunnan Paiyao is best used on small animals, it is also helpful with horses. When these high-strung animal-athletes are running under intense levels of stress, capillaries in their lungs may burst, and blood may come spewing out of the nose. The peculiar response of these horses, which are known as "bleeders," may not seriously impair their health, but it can slow their speed. So bleeders are often given a paste made up of Yunnan Paiyao before they run; it's squirted onto the tongue from a little tube. The result has been a significant decrease in bleeding problems in some horses.

Clearly, Yunnan Paiyao has enjoyed great success in overcoming a variety of animal complaints, yet it's only the first among the most effective herbs I have identified. Herbal remedy number two offers quite a different, but equally helpful, set of medical opportunities.

Remedy #2: Polyporus Combination

The origin of this herbal combination, based on various fungi, is still a mystery. More important than its origin is the fact that it works remarkably well in some cases as a substitute for antibiotics, especially to overcome chronic urinary tract problems. A pet may be brought in to see me with symptoms of blood or crystals in the urine, painful urination, or even an inability to urinate at all because of a blockage of the urinary tract. In such situations, I think of Polyporus Combination as a possible treatment.

With urinary crystals, the initial Western treatment is to administer antibiotics. But sometimes, especially with male cats, it may be necessary to anesthetize the animal and pass a catheter up the urinary tract to remove the obstacles. If the problem keeps recurring, it may even be necessary to remove the tip of the cat's penis so that the ends of the urethra can be permanently widened.

On one occasion, a four-year-old male tabby was brought in to me with a recurring urine crystallization problem. The owner had tried a number of different antibiotics and adjustments in diet, but nothing had worked. Having already paid for x-rays, urine cultures, and a variety of other tests, he said he didn't want to spend the additional several hundred dollars for the required surgery. Also, he was concerned about the discomfort the cat would have to endure with the procedure.

The owner agreed to try herbs first, and I began to give the cat a daily capsule of Polyporus Combination. Within a week the symptoms had disappeared—without any help from antibiotics. I kept the cat on this remedy for three weeks, and the condition never recurred.

As the case with antibiotics, no one particular herb or herbal formula can lay claim to being a cure-all. Rather, most herbs have very specific uses for certain diseases or conditions. So Polyporus Combination may be great for urinary tract complaints, but an upper respiratory problem requires an entirely different remedy, which leads me to the next herbal formula, Yin Chiao.

Remedy #3: Yin Chiao

In many cases, I have found that this preparation, which was first formulated by medical experts of the Ching Dynasty in China, is a remarkable remedy for influenza. Based on such ingredients as the herbs lonicera japonica and forsythia, the Yin Chiao formula can also relieve phlegm, congestion, coughing, fever, and symptoms of the common cold in humans.

I used this remedy for my own colds before trying it on my animal patients. I remember my first experience with it quite vividly. I started feeling miserable—sneezing and aching—while on my way to deliver a lecture in Kentucky. It didn't seem like an ordinary cold and, in fact, it was a nasty strain of flu that was going around that season. I had been told by others who had had it that there was nothing I could do except grin and bear it.

But then I recalled that my friend Ihor Basko had recently described some of the merits of using Yin Chiao to combat the flu, and it also dawned on me that I still had a few samples of the formula. So I began taking the tablets—about four of them twice a day. After ingesting the first group of pills, I started to feel better within an hour. By the next day, the symptoms had disappeared.

I figured if the stuff could work so well on me, there was a better than even chance it would help my animals. I got my chance to check it out when a cat was brought in to me with an upper respiratory infection and a high fever. The animal was really suffering, with coughing, a runny nasal discharge, poor appetite, and weepy eyes.

The usual treatment in cases like this was to give antibiotics to clear up any possible infections and then just let the disease run its course. As it happened, a number of antibiotics had already been tried, but nothing relieved the symptoms. The condition went on for three weeks, and the cat's weight dropped from a normal level of 11.2 pounds to 9.5. With his continuing failure to eat, it seemed inevitable that he would become even thinner. By the time the cat was referred to me, he had been tested for feline leukemia, feline AIDS, feline infectious peritonitis, and toxoplasmosis—all of which were negative.

Very concerned about their cat, the owners asked me if there were any "untested" or "alternative" treatments that might work, and I told them about Yin Chiao. They immediately decided to try the herbal approach, and I gave them the appropriate tablets with instructions about daily doses. Within forty-eight hours of receiving the first herbal treatment, the cat's temperature was back to normal and he was eating more heartily. After one week, everything cleared up, and the condition never recurred.

Another cat that belonged to a friend of mine stopped eating suddenly and developed a fever that could have been due to a protozoan parasite which causes a disease known as toxoplasmosis. This ailment, which may be spread to humans through feces in the litter pan, can often be treated with antibiotics. But that approach didn't work with my friend's cat and she continued to go downhill.

Finally, we decided to try Yin Chiao. I used the same approach that had worked with the other cat. As before, within forty-eight hours her temperature returned to normal and she started eating regularly. After seven days of herbal treatment, she was healed, and there was never a recurrence.

When using Yin Chiao, as with all herbs, it's important to be cautious. There is another remedy on the market also called Yin Chiao which contains aspirin and antihistamines. Aspirin is poisonous to cats. So do not use this herbal formula without consulting a veterinarian experienced in herbal medicine.

Although herbal remedies like Yin Chiao haven't been subjected to scientific testing to the same extent as our standard Western medicines, my clinical experience with them has revealed a certain consistency in the way they work. Remarkably, using this formula with two similar but still distinct health problems required almost exactly the same mode of treatment and resulted in a cure in similar lengths of time.

The more I have worked with herbs, the more confident I have become about discerning which diseases to use them with, and what to expect once the treatment begins.

Remedy #4: Tang-kuei 18

Chronic liver problems are a common complaint for both cats and dogs. When a German shepherd came in for treatment because of a poor appetite, dull and dry coat, flaking skin, lethargy, and depressed demeanor, I suspected her liver was the cause. She just didn't seem to be enjoying life anymore. I felt her abdomen, and sure enough, her liver was enlarged.

I ran some blood tests for liver function and discovered that the dog's liver enzymes weren't normal. Abnormal liver enzymes can be an indication of hepatitis, degenerative disease, or a malignancy. There could also have been an environmental factor, such as a toxin in the dog's food or water, that caused the liver to become inflamed.

Many treatments had already been tried, including antibiotics and low-fat, low-protein diet. But nothing had worked. Finally, a biopsy determined that even though there was no malignancy, there was a chronic degeneration of the liver, which no drugs seemed to be able to stop.

Since nothing more could be done for the animal, an herbal remedy was a last resort—specifically Tang-kuei 18, which I knew was associated with relief of liver problems. This formula, which is derived from ginseng and a variety of other herbs, is believed by the Chinese to nourish the blood, improve kidney and liver functions, and relieve abdominal pain.

So I put the shepherd on the Tang-kuei 18 in daily doses, and I could see some improvement within a few days. Her energy returned, and the condition of her coat improved. After four weeks, we rechecked her blood and found that her liver functions were returning to normal. Apparently, the herbs were helping the liver regenerate itself. In some instances, so long as there is no malignancy, the condition of a degenerative liver can be improved—and this appeared to be one of those situations.

In a somewhat different case, Mugsy, a fifteen-year-old "purebred" mutt, was brought in to me with stiff and arthritic front legs. I had already done acupuncture on Mugsy for incontinence, and the owners thought the same treatment might work for his new problem. Unfortunately, when I examined him, I discovered that what Mugsy now had was an advanced form of cancer. An ultrasound exam revealed lymphosarcoma, which had affected his liver, spleen, and pancreas. In fact, he had a tumor the size of a small melon that took up most of his abdomen—a huge malignancy for a forty-pound dog, and one that was clearly inoperable.

"At his age, we don't want to be heroic about this and put him through surgery or chemotherapy," the owners told me. "We just want to buy him a little extra time."

My own clinic colleagues and the veterinarians at the Animal Medical Center in New York felt that, at most, Mugsy might have three weeks left, and I tended to agree. So I decided to try a combination of herbal treatments with Tang-kuei 18, which would help clean out the blood, and also some glandular therapy.

Glandular therapy, like many of the other "alternative" approaches to medical care that I use, is controversial, though its use actually dates back to the sixteenth-century Swiss physician Paracelsus. I have found that in many cases it can help animals with certain problems—especially those involving vital organs like the kidney or liver. The theory behind glandular therapy is to "cure like with like." So if you have a kidney problem, you would feed the animal small amounts of food supplements derived from a kidney. Or if you have a liver complaint, you try putting more liver into the diet. In this case, I gave Mugsy a glandular supplement called "Eco Liver," which is organic liver that comes from New Zealand sheep.

The owners began to give Mugsy the Tang-kuei 18 and the glandular supplements every day, and about a month later they left a message for me to call them. I was sure they were going to report that Mugsy was dead, and I just hoped that his last days had been relatively comfortable. Instead, they said, "Boy, our dog's doing great! He's playing and running around and acting like a puppy!"

When they brought Mugsy back in for another visit, I palpated his abdomen and could feel that the tumor was still there, but it hadn't grown any bigger. Also, the dog's behavior confirmed what the owners had reported. He was obviously feeling a great deal better. I certainly didn't known where this treatment was taking us, but I was grateful to see this much of an improvement in a dog with such a large tumor. I said to the owners, "Mugsy will let you know when he's ready to leave you."

The owners agreed that they should just celebrate each additional day they could spend with their pet and let tomorrow take care of itself. Month after month went by, with Mugsy's condition staying about the same. He was enjoying life, and his owners were enjoying him. But, finally, after the eleventh month, they called and said, "Last week wasn't quite right with Mugsy. He wasn't getting up as quickly, and today, he doesn't seem to want to get up at all. Like you said, I think he's telling us he wants to let go."

A few days later, they brought Mugsy in, and I put him to sleep. But their willingness to take a chance on an unusual form of treatment—plus their constant love and affection—had been decisive in giving them an extra year with their pet.

Remedy #5: AC-Q

When a pet is having problems with rheumatoid arthritis, which is that variety of the disease related to an unbalanced immune system, the herbal formula that has been found clinically effective in some cases is known as AC-Q. Conventional medicine has little to offer other than corticosteroids.

A nine-year-old sheltie, or Shetland sheepdog, came in to me with aches, stiffness, and swelling in the wrists and elbows of his front legs. He was suffering from rheumatoid arthritis, which is common among members of this breed. Having been placed by his regular vet on cortisone, the sheltie was now also suffering side effects from the medication: he was drinking excessive amounts of water, urinating too often, and frequently experiencing an upset stomach.

His regular vet referred the dog to me for acupuncture, and that would have been an appropriate treatment. But the owner had a demanding job and coming in for the required treatments two times a week wouldn't be possible. "Is there something else we can try first?" she asked.

"Well, there is this Chinese herb that has helped relieve stiffness in the front legs," I said.

"Great. Let's try it."

So we did. I prescribed one tablet of AC-Q twice a day, and soon the swelling went down in the front legs and the sheltie began to experience significantly more mobility. When I saw him almost a year later for a checkup, even though the rheumatoid arthritis was still present, the dog was enjoying relief from the symptoms without any side effects. If the owner had gone the normal Western medical route, the next step would have been increasingly stronger drugs, including forms of chemotherapy that can have quite serious side effects, such as kidney failure and liver disease.

But even as I describe such success stories, I want to emphasize once again that herbal remedies in the wrong hands can be toxic and extremely harmful to your pet's health. It's essential before you try herbs that you are certain that the veterinarian you are working with has training both in applying herbal remedies and in using them on your particular type of pet. Otherwise, the herbs may do your pet more harm than good.

Remedy #6: Restorative Tablets

In traditional Chinese medicine, the remedy known as Restorative Tablets, which contains a wide array of herbal components, was used to treat human complaints related to aging or to restore health after an illness. The ancient herbal practitioners claimed that these herbs nourished the "yin," or interior forces and fluids of the body. This treatment was also frequently prescribed for excessive sweating, backache, dry skin, fevers, general weakness, and menopausal symptoms.

In recommending Restorative Tablets in smaller doses for animals, I have focused on problems related to general weakness that affects some pets as they grow older, or to difficulties encountered while recovering from surgery. One thirteen-year-old dog underwent surgery to have some fatty cysts removed from his back, but he just didn't bounce back after the operation. I checked the thyroid gland and did a number of other tests, but nothing emerged as a clear cause of his problem. He continued to appear lethargic and depressed.

These symptoms persisted for about two weeks, and finally, after deciding that none of the traditional approaches were working, I suggested Restorative Tablets. Within a week of taking this prescription, the dog completely recovered his old energy.

Would the dog have recovered anyway? Probably, say the skeptics. This is often an argument offered against the effectiveness of the herbal approach to treatment. But I have seen too many cases in which pets have been unable to recover with more familiar Western treatments—or with no treatment at all—but have then snapped back quickly with Restorative Tablets.

The reasons that such herbal treatments work are not entirely clear. But research into this area is continuing, and currently at least four active chemical components have been identified in herbal remedies that may play a role in the healing process. These include polysaccharides, or long-chain sugars; alkaloids, which provide a sedative action and pain relief; flavonoids, which help bolster the immune system; and various steroidal compounds, which do not have the potential side effects of steroidal drugs. Whatever the precise scientific reasons for the action of Restorative Tablets and other herbal remedies, I can only conclude from my clinical experience that frequently they do succeed, many times where more "scientific" medicine fails.

176 HEALING

Remedy #7: Ginseng and Royal Bee Jelly

Ginseng is probably the most familiar Chinese herb. (Actually there are many different types of ginseng.) Sometimes the herb is used alone; frequently it is used in combination with other remedies. For example, the very first herbal remedy I described was Yunnan Paiyao, which consists largely of tien chi ginseng, an herb that promotes clotting of blood. Then there is Siberian ginseng, which is known to increase the leukocytes, the white blood cells that fight infection, inhibit tumor growth, and perform other immune functions. Ginseng is usually taken in combination with other herbs, though when taken alone, it can act almost like pure caffeine, as a powerful stimulant.

Ginseng can work well in combination with royal bee jelly to fight the effects of feline leukemia, a devastating disease that can take a cat's life in a matter of a few weeks or months. Together, the ginseng and the royal bee jelly act to stimulate the immune system and the animal's appetite.

The royal bee jelly, which is the finest that can be found in a beehive, is used like an herb in this particular formula. Even though the source of the jelly is animal rather than plant, the Chinese don't hesitate to use it. They draw on substances throughout the natural kingdom, without worrying too much about whether they are flora or fauna. The main thing they look for is the mixture that does the best job of healing. Personally, however, I do not support the use of parts of endangered species, such as tiger bone or bear gallbladder, in Chinese herbal formulas. Modern herbalists are currently finding substitutes for these objectionable components.

How well does the ginseng–royal bee jelly concoction really work? Consider a patient of mine, a seven-year-old, black-and-white female shorthair who was suffering from feline leukemia. The cat belonged to a single woman who relished her pet's companionship and couldn't bear the thought of her being sick or dying. But despite the application of many conventional Western treatments, the cat had grown weaker and weaker. Also, she had frequent fevers, a loss of appetite, and declining weight. In short, she was dying.

When the failing feline was brought in to me, the first alternative therapy I tried was acupuncture. That worked to some extent for a while; her appetite improved and the fevers decreased. But then the cat's condition worsened, and I decided to try some herbs. The ginseng and the royal bee jelly came in liquid form, in a product called Ginseng Royal Jelly, and so I prescribed six drops three times a day. Immediately, the very first day, the cat's energy levels began to improve.

The cat never overcame her feline leukemia; the disease is incurable and is generally thought to be terminal. But despite the fact that the cat continued to test positive for leukemia, her symptoms disappeared and the disease went into remission. When I again heard from the owner seven years later, she said, "My cat's just gone out of remission and is real sick and feverish."

"Are you still giving her the herbal formula?" I asked.

"No. I stopped a few years ago because she was doing so well."

I told her to bring the cat into my office for a checkup, and when they arrived, I prescribed more of the ginseng and royal bee jelly remedy. Although the cat did bounce back to good health, before long she suffered another relapse from which there was no recovery. But the herbal formula had succeeded in keeping her alive and symptom-free for nearly eight years—even though she was suffering from a tremendously debilitating, fatal disease!

Remedy #8: Astragalus 10-Plus

This herbal formula, whose main ingredient comes from the root of the astragalus plant, has the ability to strengthen immune functions, but it works in a somewhat different way from other herbs. Astragalus is often referred to as an "adaptogen" because it enhances many bodily functions while increasing the effectiveness of other herbs in the compound; these additional herbs help overcome chronic infections that ordinary antibiotics are unable to treat.

An elderly woman brought in her fourteen-year-old terrier

for an evaluation because of complications that had developed from the animal's bad teeth. Undergoing dental surgery for infections that had spread to the roots of his teeth, the dog had been placed on strong antibiotics, and his most recent blood tests had come back normal. But he still suffered from infections on a regular basis. One week it would be a skin problem. Then an ear would erupt. Then an upper respiratory problem would develop, accompanied by a cough.

"He just seems so exhausted," the owner said.

Indeed, the terrier was in a run-down condition, primarily because his immune system was chronically weak. So the first thing I thought about was Astragalus 10-Plus. I prescribed it, and little by little the dog's symptoms subsided and his energy returned. Nor was he getting those recurrent infections anymore. The herbs had been able to intervene where antibiotics had fallen short, enabling the dog's immune system to recover.

Another terrier, a gray-and-white twelve-year-old, was suffering from a chronic discharge of pus from one nostril, and no one seemed able to figure out the source of the problem. Her regular veterinarian had placed her on antibiotics, which helped to some extent. But the nasal discharge continued. X-rays had failed to reveal any abscess or mass that might be causing the pus. Then the dog was referred to a surgeon, who did exploratory surgery to see if there might be a tumor, foreign object, or fungus that the x-rays hadn't picked up. But still nothing.

After four months of undergoing all these tests and treatments, the terrier was referred to me as sort of a last-gasp effort before being put to sleep. It would seem that I had developed a reputation as the vet of last resort!

The first time I saw the dog, her prospects didn't look too bright. But I began a dual treatment of acupuncture and Chinese herbs, specifically Astragalus 10-Plus. I used the acupuncture to open the sinuses and stimulate the immune system. Then I employed the herbs to bolster the immune system still further. The discharge from the nose seemed to me to indicate a general failure of the dog's immune system, and Astragalus 10-Plus is often an effective remedy.

Immediately after the first acupuncture session—which involved inserting a needle in the master point between the toes of the left front paw that correspond to our thumb and index finger—the discharge came pouring out of the dog's nose in even greater quantities than before. That was precisely the initial result I had hoped for because it was essential for the sinuses to be cleaned out before the herbs could do their work properly.

With the combined treatment of acupuncture and herbs, the terrier began to feel much better almost immediately. She managed to fall asleep before she arrived home after our first session and continued to sleep for about twenty-four hours. When she awoke, the discharge was already clearing up. After four treatments with the herbs, the discharge disappeared almost completely.

I realized that the herbs were the most important component of the treatment because when we tapered off the acupuncture after a few days, the dog continued to do well. On the other hand, when I stopped the herbs, the infections gradually returned. The terrier stayed on the herbal remedy for the next two years and finally died of heart failure at age fourteen. But she had had no further problems with the nasal discharge.

Remedy #9: Valerian

Another exception to the general rule that herbs normally work best for smaller animals like cats and dogs is the use of the ninth and last remedy, the herb valerian, which can be just what the vet needs to calm an agitated equine. Valerian, which grows naturally in the United States, Africa, Great Britain, and various other locations around the globe, has long been used by herbal healers to calm jittery nerves, cure insomnia, and relieve general irritability. To produce these effects, the herb is often combined with other herbs, such as skullcap, mistletoe, or peppermint. The roots of the valerian plant, which is commonly known as the garden heliotrope, are the the central ingredient in the formula I used with agitated horses.

Because horses make up a substantial part of my veterinary

practice, I have gotten to know their personality traits and those of their owners rather well. It is not unusual for horses to reflect the personalities of the people who surround them. One extremely successful executive seemed to expect the same high level of performance from his mare as he did from his employees. It was not that he treated the animal unkindly. On the contrary, he doted on the mare as he doted on his own daughters, giving her the highest-quality feed, attentive grooming, and the best accommodations. But I believe that if his exacting standards when he was riding the animal—expecting her to be near-perfect in dressage, jumping, and other skills—were not met, he somehow communicated his disappointment to her.

I was called to check on the horse because the owner thought she was too nervous and agitated. When he rode her, she seemed unable to concentrate and would sometimes break into a run, shy away from harmless objects on the ground, or even buck slightly. After evaluating the horse's physical condition, as well as her shoeing, saddle fit, and training routine, I ended up prescribing relatively small doses of valerian root with skullcap in a mixture of other herbs. At first, this remedy didn't seem to be making a difference, so I increased the dosage slightly and the horse grew calmer. After several more adjustments in the dosage, her nervousness and agitation disappeared entirely. That achieved, I slowly eased off on the herbs until I could discontinue them entirely.

Now the mare could fully live up to her owner's expectations. I was happy to have calmed her, but in my heart of hearts I wished I hadn't had to. The real problem, I felt, was that she was being unfairly held to such high standards.

There are many other herbs that have proved to have effective healing powers in cultures all over the world. For example, there is raspberry, which has been used in Europe and North America since the 1500s as a cure for diarrhea and other bowel problems. Or there is Isatis 6, an herbal formula derived from the leaf and root of the woad plant in the mustard family, which

I have found to be effective for many chronic viral infections. Or I might place an animal on licorice root with a combination of other herbs as an antidote for lack of energy.

There is often some overlap among the uses of different herbs, and I have found that with some animals several different herbal remedies may be equally helpful. On the other hand, some animals respond best to one specific remedy—in the same way we might respond best to one antibiotic. So it's necessary, by a process of careful evaluation, to find the herbal remedy that will most effectively fit the needs of a given pet. The effort is usually well spent. When conventional Western medical responses fail and we can nevertheless provide relief, we should feel deep gratitude.

CHAPTER ELEVEN

Breaking Bread with All God's Creatures

Qui me amat, amet et canem meum. *(Love me, love my dog.)*

—St. Bernard, "Sermo Primus" (A.D. 1150)

So often, I hear pet owners say, "Let's feed the cat—then we can sit down to eat." Or, "Wait a minute—I have to open a can for the dog. Then we can have our talk." Or, "Quit begging, Spot, and let us eat. You've already had your meal."

The assumption is that there is a time, place, and type of meal appropriate for animals, and an entirely different set of circumstances appropriate for human nutrition—and never the twain shall meet. Actually, however, increasing numbers of pet owners are discovering that they can eat with their pets *and* enjoy similar foods together. In short, what many animals need for good nutrition is not that different from what we need. It's just a matter of making a few minor adjustments in an animal's menu and then sitting down to break bread together —and to enjoy still another opportunity to have a close relationship with your pet.

Perhaps the best starting point for this joint eating experience is to practice what I call "feeding with a loving touch." When you offer food to your dog or cat, it's important to do so with an attitude of love and care. Communicate by talking gently to your pet as you place the food before him. Tell him that you care for him, and that this food is one way you have of expressing your compassion.

One cat owner I knew began talking to her Siamese in a low, soothing tone as she was preparing her food. She would say,

"Rascal, I know you're going to love this special dish I've made for you. You like this kind of fish, and you like the sauce that goes with it. And it's so *good* for you too!"

I'm not sure the cat understood the exact words, but I do know that the message of love, as corny or saccharine as it may sound to some ears, was communicated clearly. Siamese can be rather reserved, standoffish pets. But this one apparently began to associate her owner's caring tone of voice with the good food she was about to receive. One quantifiable result was a noticeable increase in the animal's expressions of affection, an increased eagerness to nuzzle and cuddle.

Of course, this owner did not try to rub, caress, or otherwise touch her pet as she ate—and you shouldn't either. If you do, instead of eliciting an expression of love you may be greeted with a hiss, growl, or snap. But it's fine to sit quietly together. Another option, for those who are spiritually or religiously inclined, is to spend some time in prayer or meditation as your pet eats. Creating a quiet, meditative environment can do wonders to calm your cat or dog and enhance his digestive process. One pet owner, who was in the habit of spending about a half hour each day in prayer and meditation, organized her schedule so that this spiritual discipline could be exercised at the same time her dog was eating. As part of her meditation, she devoted several minutes to focusing on her pet's health and to searching for creative ways to enhance his overall well-being. This symbolic "breaking of the bread" can, in a very real sense, serve as a kind of communion.

To draw your pet into an expansive circle of love, you might arrange your meals so that he eats along with you or your family. Exposure to a convivial atmosphere at mealtime can be especially helpful for a pet that is a finicky eater. Just seeing other friends enjoying themselves and eating heartily at the table can greatly stimulate the animal's appetite. Several of my feline patients that seemed to have made a career out of turning their noses up at their food actually started to show considerably more interest in eating when they were fed at the same time as their human families. Venus, a haughty Persian breed, would typically eat less than half the food her owner put before her. But when her meal schedule was changed to allow her to eat with all five human members of her family, she regularly cleaned her bowl.

Once you establish the right time and place for your special animal to eat, the next step is to recognize that he needs a full array of nutrients, just as you do. Missing one key vitamin or mineral can jeopardize the health of your animal, with disastrous results. Consider what happened to a barnful of cows I was called in to examine a few years ago.

THE MIRACLE OF THE COWS

The farmer was in a panic. His cows were getting sick and dying, and nothing had been able to stop it. One after the other, they came down with some ailment—an abscess in the foot, an infection in the mouth, difficulty in calving. Then they would go off feed and, finally, die.

It seemed as though some sort of plague had descended on these cows. But what was it? Their regular veterinarian had been treating the individual symptoms, but he could find no common thread running through their ailments that would suggest an epidemic. Yet the health of the herd seemed to be getting worse.

My first thought was that there *had* to be a common thread. "It almost sounds as if there's some kind of nutritional deficiency that's affecting your whole herd," I told the farmer. "They may be lacking something important in their food that's decreasing their resistance and preventing them from fighting off disease."

So I went out to the barn and began taking blood samples to see if the cows were low in any enzyme, vitamin, mineral, or other substance. The lab called me back within days and provided the answer. The cows were low in selenium, a very important trace mineral, an antioxidant that plays an important role in the body's processing of vitamin E and in various cellular functions. Without sufficient selenium, the cows might be suffering from a weakened immune system—and a reduced ability to fight off whatever was attacking them.

I knew that the hay in that area was notoriously low in certain nutrients, including selenium; so the results of the blood tests made eminent sense to me. I directed the farmer to begin to supplement the cows' regular diet with selenium. Within a couple of weeks, the health problems that had been afflicting the herd cleared up—and the farmer became convinced that he had witnessed a major miracle. This "miracle of the cows" was just a case of good, balanced nutrition.

I have become increasingly amazed at how some of the latest findings in human nutrition apply equally well to animals. I'll never forget Goldie, a golden retriever who had been abused by a former owner and then had been put up for adoption by the Humane Society. Soon after the new owners took Goldie into their home, she developed bone cancer and had to undergo an amputation of her front left leg. The prognosis wasn't good. But the owners didn't want to put the dog through any chemotherapy. Instead, they decided to try an "anti-cancer diet" that I suggested, in the hope that the progress of the cancer might be retarded, even if only for a brief time.

I put Goldie on home-cooked vegetables and an impressive array of vitamin supplements. As a matter of fact, the diet I suggested was quite similar to the kinds of meals that the owners had started making for themselves to reduce their own risk of cancer and heart disease. Specifically, I recommended vegetables like carrots and broccoli for high amounts of vitamin C and beta carotene. I also prescribed megadose supplements of vitamin C—up to 2000 milligrams a day. And I added vitamin E—400 International Units (IU) twice a day. Finally, I told the owners to give Goldie a multivitamin supplement that was high in B.

Also, at my suggestion, they eliminated red meat from her diet completely and substituted organic chicken. I recommend that any pet who is in a high-risk category for cancer be taken off red meat.

The medical prognosis for this particular dog wasn't too promising, however. The cancer seemed to have progressed to a point where Goldie would at best have a few months left to live. But I figured that the diet and vitamin regimen couldn't hurt, and it might buy the dog a little time.

As it turned out, the owners moved away and I lost track of them. But five years later, when I was in the Humane Society offices examining another dog that was about to be adopted, one of the society officials asked, "You remember that dog Goldie, with the cancer that required an amputation?"

"Sure," I said.

"Well, that dog is still alive!"

Goldie's wasn't an isolated phenomenon in my experience. The same good nutrition that works for you will result in improved behavior, energy, and overall health in your pet.

SHOULD ANIMALS TRY A HUMAN DIET?

Many of our lethal illnesses can be directly linked to a poor diet. If *you* eat a low-fiber, high-fat diet rather than healthy food, you're much more likely to come down with colon cancer or heart disease. Animals have several of the same problems. Some commercial pet food products are made from what I call the "three Ds"—already dead, diseased, or dying animals. They contain too many hormones, too many antibiotics, and too much rotting, tumorous flesh. This stuff has been condemned for human consumption, yet we allow it to be made into pet food. But with a properly designed diet for your pet— and for the most part, this means a homemade diet that would, with a few adjustments, be suitable for humans—you can eliminate the three Ds and simultaneously reduce the risk of cancer, heart disease, and other ills.

What are the main ingredients of a good pet diet? Like a healthy human diet, your pet's diet should above all emphasize foods that are (1) high in fiber, (2) lower in fat, and (3) organically grown.

The High-Fiber Factor

I always suggest that for dogs one-half of the *portions* (not the calories) of their daily diet consist of high-fiber foods such as whole grain brown rice, oatmeal, millet, barley, or quinoa. About 20 percent of the daily diet should consist of vegetables and fruits, which also tend to be high in fiber. Only about 30 percent should consist of meat, fish, or poultry.

As for cats, I recommend that about 20 percent of their daily food allotment come from high-fiber grains like cooked brown rice, millet, and quinoa, and another 20 percent from vegetables. Sixty percent of the helpings should be animal protein sources, like meat, poultry, and fish.

Cats need more animal products than dogs because they are more complete carnivores than their canine cousins, and they naturally prefer to eat more meat. Also, cats on average tend to have higher calorie requirements, pound for pound, than dogs, and animal foods, which contain more fats, can supply those extra calories. (A given weight of fat contains about twice the amount of calories as a comparable weight of carbohydrate or protein.)

But these high calorie demands have a price. They may cause owners to forget that fiber must always be a full partner with fat in their pets' meals. Animals that subsist solely on some commercial cat and dog foods are getting insufficient portions of high-fiber vegetables and grains. Adequate fiber is essential in enabling a pet to maintain a healthy gastrointestinal system.

A bull mastiff named Hoagie was brought in to me because of complaints about his bowel movements. Ever since he was a puppy, he had been suffering from chronic, watery diarrhea. Vet after vet had tried different therapeutic approaches, including special prescription diets and heavy doses of cortisone. A series of biopsies of the intestine had revealed that the dog was suffering from gastroenteritis, an inflammation of the stomach and intestinal tract, but nothing seemed to relieve his symptoms. In fact, he grew worse. Hoagie started drinking more, urinating more, and becoming more irritable and anxious.

I took one look at his diet—an inferior brand of commercial dog food—and decided that his body was literally crying out for more quality fiber. So I placed him on a rotating diet of millet, sweet potatoes, and other high-fiber, nutrient-rich foods. Usually, high-fiber foods are used to overcome constipation, but I have found that they often work just as well to stabilize chronic diarrhea. In addition to the dietary change, I employed some acupuncture and treatments with Chinese herbs to help enhance the dog's immune system.

Sure enough, within six months Hoagie was bounding into my office completely cured of his intestinal problems. His energy levels had increased dramatically, and he continued to enjoy life as an entirely new dog—primarily because of the introduction of more fiber into his daily diet.

The Fat Factor

The one place where an animal diet usually differs markedly from a human diet is in the need for fats. Even though the fat in your pet's diet should probably be lower than what he's now getting, cats and dogs generally need more fat than humans because their calorie needs are greater. That is why I have recommended that the average cat receive about 60 percent of his daily food portions from animal sources, and the average dog about 30 percent. Very active dogs or those with a high metabolism should get a higher proportion of animal foods— say 35–40 percent of their total daily intake.

One extremely active, bouncy terrier always became increasingly irritable late in the day, just before his second meal. His owner had to keep him away from children or guests at those times because he was likely to take a nip out of someone if he was handled too much. As it turned out, all this dog needed was a few more calories late in the afternoon to keep his energy up and his emotions on a more even keel. This was achieved by giving him a meat snack in the middle of the afternoon, or sometimes just by adding some extra meat to his morning meal. With the additional calories provided by the saturated fat in this food, the terrier calmed down and became a much more congenial companion.

The meats you choose for saturated fats, proteins, and other nutrients should include the heart, kidney, spleen, and liver. Organically raised lamb and chicken, as well as fish (without bones), such as catfish, carp, salmon, tuna, or haddock, provide good, tasty possibilities. You can usually find the organic types of food by examining the packaging labels. Serving these foods raw will provide the most nutrients. But to be completely safe about eliminating any bacteria or parasites, I would recommend that the meats and other animal products be lightly steamed or boiled.

Despite the need most pets have for meat, for some allergic dogs and cats, red meats such as beef or lamb may have to be eliminated entirely. And some highly allergic dogs may have to be placed on a tightly supervised, *totally* vegetarian diet—without even any fish or chicken. A rotation diet may also be necessary for allergic dogs. This involves rotating foods every few days so that the dog does not develop allergies to the current food source. This should be monitored by your veterinarian.

Here are a couple of vegetarian suggestions. Tofu, a form of bean curd, can be a good high-protein substitute for meat. Also, you can get extra protein from yogurt—the only dairy product I regard as acceptable for most pets—and from a boiled egg a couple of times a week.

What about fish oils? The same benefits from fish oils that are enjoyed by humans are also available to your pets. So when you prepare fish for yourself, include an extra helping for your pet.

The best sources of these oils, known as "omega-3 fatty acids," are herring, salmon, bluefish, and tuna. Fish oil can also be obtained through supplements, but I don't recommend this approach unless you pursue it under the watchful eye of your veterinarian. It's too easy to ingest an overdose of omega-3 oils through pills, which would put your pet at risk for internal bleeding. But taken in judicious amounts through the diet, these fish oils may protect your cat or dog against heart disease and high blood pressure, ease the discomforts of arthritis, and provide a number of the same benefits they provide for you.

The Organic Factor

When you choose vegetables, grains, fruits, meats, or other foods, your preference should be for those that are labeled *organically grown*—meaning those that are not treated with pesticides, hormones, or other chemicals. Too many important nutrients are eliminated during processing or tainted by chemicals, and the result may be serious health problems for your pet.

Like a number of other veterinarians, I had a close encounter a number of years ago with the dangers of processed foods when some of my cat patients experienced mysterious heart failure. It was happening to hundreds of other cats around the country, and an investigation determined that a deficiency of taurine, an essential amino acid, was the cause. This particular nutrient had been completely processed out of the meat in many commercial cat foods.

Now, some cat food products claim to be "fortified with taurine," but that doesn't give me much confidence. They may have taken care of the taurine problem, but what about the deficiencies in other nutrients, which we won't find out about until other symptoms appear? I prefer to stick with homemade foods or high-quality prepared foods packed with the maximum possible nutritional value.

There are a number of ways to tell whether an animal is getting good home cooking based on organically grown ingredients. These animals have beautiful, healthy, shiny coats, and no offensive body odor. Their skin is clear and moist, not dry, flaky, or inflamed. Also, there is no buildup of wax in their ears.

The impact of organic foods can go well beyond mere outward appearance, however. These products may actually make the difference between health and illness, or even life and death. One German shepherd developed chronic problems with itching and infections of the skin. Nothing seemed to work until we placed him on a home-cooked, organic vegetarian diet, with an emphasis on foods like broccoli, corn, and yams. Almost immediately after going on this diet, the dog's skin problems cleared up. And little by little, we were able to reintroduce meat.

This shepherd's recovery echoed the experience of another patient of mine, a twelve-year-old black Labrador owned by the actor Dustin Hoffman. The dog had cancer, a tumor of the thyroid gland, and when he was first brought in to see me, he could barely breathe because the tumor, which was twelve inches long, was pressing against the windpipe just beneath the skin, like a big, deadly cucumber. The only way he could take in air was to open his mouth wide and gulp, and that made him cough and sputter.

The prognosis wasn't good. Other veterinarians had suggested that the dog be put to sleep immediately, and the maximum time they gave him to live was four to six weeks. I could see that it was probably useless for me to try to cure a malignancy that far advanced. So my goal was just to try to do what I could to make the animal's life a little easier.

I used various herbs, but another important line of attack was nutritional. I put the dog almost entirely on a diet of lightly cooked grains and vegetables, including millet, carrots, broccoli, green beans, and zucchini. Everything was fresh and organically grown; nothing was processed. This Labrador could never be a complete vegetarian, but he could be taken off red meat. To provide adequate protein, I gave him fresh fish and turkey.

The results were gratifying. After two months of treatment— a period that had already exceeded the animal's predicted life span since the time I first saw him—he was doing much better. He could breathe easily and was behaving in a livelier fashion. He had so much more energy that he actually liked to play! After six months of treatment, he was still happy and playful. While I couldn't expect this dog's cancer to be cured, something significant and beneficial was happening to him that would prolong his life.

My own clinical experience with the benefits of organic foods is increasingly being backed up by broader scientific studies. In a recent investigation done in Chicago at the Doctors' Data Laboratory and reported in the *Journal of Applied Nutrition,* researcher Bob L. Smith reported that on an ounce-for-ounce basis, organic fruits and vegetables are twice as rich in important micronutrients as commercial products. He compared commercial and organically grown pears, apples, sweet corn, potatoes, and wheat samples. Among other things, Smith found that in the organic foods, in contrast to the commercial products, there was

- 390 percent more selenium, which is important for the immune system and muscle strength
- 178 percent more manganese, which is important for nerve and muscle development
- 138 percent more magnesium, which plays a key role in healthy heart functioning
- 125 percent more potassium, which helps muscle development and maintenance

Also, the organic foods were considerably lower than the commercial products in toxic substances, such as aluminum, lead, and mercury.

As important as it is to give pets the best possible diet, many of us are so busy these days that we don't have time to cook for ourselves, let alone for our furry companions. If you find yourself in that position, don't feel guilty about what you can't do. Instead, throw your energies into finding a commercial dog or cat food that is loaded with natural, high-quality ingredients. You should avoid those that are made up mostly of meat by-products (which include beaks, feathers, intestines, tumors, feet, and hoofs). If your pet has a tendency toward allergies, you should also avoid products that include wheat, red meat, or corn. Do look for pet foods with meat or grains labeled "organically grown," or for those made up of "human grade" food products. And of course, just because one pet food is more expensive does not mean it is the best. For your pet's sake, read the labels carefully.

If your lifestyle affords you the opportunity to plan and cook meals for your pet, I have designed some model menus: "Food Fit for a Dog" and "A Cat's Repast." You can use these menus as a starting point to enlarge your pet's nutritional vistas. Keep in mind that no matter what you feed your pet, you should serve it in a porcelain or stainless-steel bowl, since many animals are allergic to the dyes in plastic.

FOOD FIT FOR A DOG

The first of the following meal suggestions involves a one-day menu for your dog, and the second is a proposal for bulk preparation of several meals. These foods can be taken directly off your own table if you find the particular ones I have chosen to your own liking. Although I have made some cooking suggestions, the precise way you fix these foods will be left up to your own taste and that of your pet. You will have to experiment to see which approaches to food preparation turn on his taste buds, and which cause him to walk away from his bowl after half-eating the food or just giving it a few sniffs.

Let me offer a few caveats before you actually go into the kitchen. Animal diets must be adjusted according to age, stress levels, exercise habits, food allergies, and health conditions like diabetes, pancreatitis, or colitis. I'm assuming with these model menus that your pet is generally in good health, that he participates in average levels of physical activity, and that he's under no particular stress in your household. Animals that are extremely active or under great stress tend to have higher calorie needs.

Also, a word about dog weight. Usually, the larger your dog, the more calories he requires. Here are some general guidelines as to the number of pounds of homemade food that dogs of different weights should be served each day:

Body Weight	Approximate Daily Amount
5–10 pounds	½ pound
20 pounds	1 pound
40 pounds	1½ pounds
60 pounds	2 pounds
80–100 pounds	2½ pounds

These amounts of food may be given to the dog once a day or divided between two meals. But you should never let your dog eat as much as he wants throughout the day. If you do, you'll be opening the door to canine obesity. Instead, offer him his meal for ten or fifteen minutes, and then remove any uneaten portion. At the corresponding meal the next day, give him the same amount consumed at this meal. He should consume just enough each day to maintain his normal body weight —which should be determined by your veterinarian.

In general, meats and vegetables should be mixed in the morning meal, and grains and vegetables in the evening meal. But if you find your pet doesn't like to eat grains and vegetables without meat, it's all right to serve meat at both meals.

Dog Menu: One Day

¼ pound diced fish or lean organic meat, such as lamb, chicken, chicken liver, heart, or kidney. Boil or broil lightly—or prepare otherwise, as you and your dog prefer.

1 cup flaked oats, rye, or barley soaked in water. Occasionally you may add baked potatoes or sweet potatoes. These components may be mixed together or prepared as a single dish.

1 teaspoon organic cold-pressed flaxseed oil. Do not heat or cook.

¼ cup grated or chopped organic vegetables, such as carrots, broccoli, and zucchini. These should be served raw or steamed lightly.

1 teaspoon organic apple cider vinegar.

Multivitamin/mineral supplement.

1 tablespoon kelp meal.

1 teaspoon minced garlic.

The yield for this menu is approximately three-quarters of a pound of food, or enough for a fifteen-pound dog. Adjust the amount up or down according to your dog's weight, in line with the guidelines given on the chart opposite.

Make the transition gradually from commercial dog food to a homemade diet. The first week you can serve your dog a portion that's three-quarters of the old diet and one-quarter of the new. The second week, serve portions that are one-half new diet and one-half old. The third week, the portions should equal three-quarters new diet and one-quarter old. Finally, by the fourth week, your pet can eat a full diet of the new food.

If you fix some variation of this basic menu for yourself, you will undoubtedly want to serve the items separately and in different proportions, with more of an emphasis on the vegetables and grains and less on the animal products. But for your pet, it will probably be most appetizing to mix all these items together well. Also, keep the food covered in the refrigerator if you don't plan to serve it immediately. The vegetables, by themselves, make great treats or snacks rather than junk food.

You can multiply these amounts by five or more in order to make a large supply in advance. Divide the food into one-day portions, place each into a foil-covered bowl or sealable plastic bag, and refrigerate.

Dog Menu: Multiple Days

3 cups diced lean organic meat—such as lamb, chicken, chicken liver, heart, or kidney—or salmon or deboned catfish. Boil or broil lightly.

15 cups flaked oats, rye, or barley soaked in water. Occasionally you may add baked potatoes or sweet potatoes.

2 tablespoons organic cold-pressed flaxseed oil. Do not heat or cook.

2 cups grated or chopped organic vegetables, such as carrots, green beans, zucchini, and broccoli. Serve them raw or lightly steamed.

The yield from this recipe is about 20 cups, or enough food for about three days for a seventy-pound dog. Serve at room temperature and sprinkle a multivitamin/mineral supplement over the food at each feeding.

A CAT'S REPAST

In preparing your cat's daily meal, you should plan on giving him more animal protein foods—such as meats, poultry, and fish—than you would a dog. Specifically, about 60 percent of your cat's daily intake should consist of animal protein sources, 20 percent should be vegetables, and 20 percent should be grains.

Each cat will have his own individual preferences about types of meat, fish, grain, or vegetables. The cat may seem to go for fish more than other types of animal protein. But you should be sure not to give fish as his only protein source because your cat needs more nutritional balance than this. Also, some fish may be tainted by pollution, and excessive helpings can have a negative impact on your pet's health. As with dogs, make sure to make the transition gradually from a commercial diet to home-cooked meals.

The amounts of food can be served according to the guidelines below, depending on the weight of your cat:

Body Weight	Approximate Daily Amount
7 pounds	¾ cup
10 pounds	1 cup
12 pounds	1¼ cup

If your cat is larger than twelve pounds, you should feed him more, but adjust the portions so that he maintains his ideal weight, as determined by the veterinarian. Avoid letting your cat become obese.

Cat Menu: One Day

⅔ cup organic lamb, chicken, or fish, or organ meat such as heart, liver, or kidney. Boil, broil, or steam lightly.

⅛ cup medium-cooked organically produced eggs.

⅙ cup grated organic carrots, broccoli, squash, sweet potatoes, and zucchini. Steam lightly or serve raw.

⅙ cup cooked brown rice, millet, oatmeal, or quinoa.

⅛ teaspoon organic cold-pressed flaxseed oil. Do not heat or cook.

⅛ teaspoon kelp.

Touch of minced garlic.

This menu should provide about the right amount for a ten-pound cat. Adjust portion up or down according to your pet's weight.

Cat Menu: Multiple Days

3 cups organic lamb, chicken, or fish, or organ meat such as heart, liver, or kidney. Boil, broil, or steam lightly.

2 medium-cooked organically produced eggs.

1 cup grated organic carrots, broccoli, squash, sweet potatoes, and zucchini. Steam lightly or serve raw.

1 cup cooked brown rice, millet, oatmeal, or quinoa.

1 teaspoon organic cold-pressed flaxseed oil. Do not heat or cook.

½ teaspoon kelp.

¼ teaspoon minced garlic.

This preparation will yield just over five cups, which you should chop and mix up thoroughly. Then, for a ten-pound cat, divide it into five sealable plastic bags or foil packages and refrigerate. Serve each package as one meal or two separate meals each day, adding a multivitamin/mineral supplement daily. If your cat is smaller or larger than ten pounds, adjust the amounts of each meal in line with the guidelines suggested on page 196.

. . .

By paying closer attention to your pet's nutrition, you can play a direct role in extending his life and ensuring that he is able to live every day to the fullest. What's more, by "feeding with a loving touch," you will discover that food can be more than a routine necessity of life. For you and your pet, meals can become a transcendent time to share.

CHAPTER TWELVE

A Homeopathic Medicine Chest

The important thing is not to stop questioning.

—ALBERT EINSTEIN

An animal "talent agency" was in the throes of a crisis with its star camel, Camille, which was booked for the Radio City Christmas show in New York City. Camille had been tackled by another camel during a lively recreation period. She fell to the floor and couldn't get up, despite intense cajoling and coaxing from her trainer. As a result of the attack, Camille suffered a serious injury to her leg, and the woman who owned the agency, fearing that her star had a fracture, telephoned me from Manhattan and asked what they should do.

"You've got to find out if there's really a break," I said. "That means an x-ray, fluoroscope, or similar procedure."

They managed to get Camille into the office of the one veterinarian I thought of whose space could accommodate the animal, but he couldn't keep the agitated desert-bred prima donna still long enough to take accurate pictures. There was some evidence of a fracture, so the owner called me again. "Look, we just want you to check the leg," she said. "If you feel it, perhaps you could tell if there's a break. Can you possibly come to New York?"

I agreed to come if they would take Camille to a farm where I regularly saw horses. So the camel was transported by trailer and was waiting there for my examination the next day. At our first meeting, I knew I wasn't going to be dealing with a sweet, docile patient. I heard Camille snorting and spitting even before I laid eyes on her. Then when I tried to execute a cautious approach toward her leg, she wouldn't let me near her.

Finally, after about five minutes of squirming and spitting, Camille calmed down enough for me to move in and feel the leg. There was a fracture, all right. Fortunately, the bones appeared to be in place.

"It would help if you could have her operated on to enable the bones to knit properly," I advised.

But the owner objected. "Another camel of mine had a more serious fracture and had to have an operation. He got sick from the antibiotics, developed kidney failure, and died."

Since surgery obviously wasn't acceptable, and because the bones appeared to be stable and in alignment, I concluded that the best alternative was to let the camel heal by herself— with the aid of a homeopathic remedy, symphytum officinale, a minute dilution of the comfrey plant. As always, I explained that homeopathy, which involves the use of extreme dilutions of plant, mineral, and animal products, is regarded as an unconventional method of treatment by mainstream veterinary groups. Still, I told the owner that many veterinarians have found homeopathic remedies work quite well with certain animal health conditions, and comfrey is one of those substances that medical practitioners have relied on since ancient times. In fact, comfrey was known by the term "knit bone" among Native American medicine men because, as the name implies, it was used to hasten the healing of fractures.

The owner agreed to try the treatment, and so I prescribed a solution of symphytum at twice the human dosage and directed her to squirt the remedy onto the camel's tongue daily. Also, I prescribed another homeopathic remedy, arnica montana, to reduce the pain and swelling from the injury.

Regardless of the medical technique employed, early treatment of such an injury in a relatively large animal is always a tricky business. The handlers would have to keep Camille quiet so that the leg wouldn't be reinjured or the broken bones knocked out of place. At the same time, however, they would have to move all her limbs regularly to prevent muscle atrophy.

The healing process in this case involved exceptionally large doses of patience and compassion—and a willingness to put up with a particularly irascible theatrical temperament. But perseverance paid off. Camille's owner was ecstatic about her star's recovery and rather surprised by how well the unusual treatment had worked. As for me, I had become accustomed over the years to watching homeopathic medicines succeed where other treatments failed. But I hadn't always been that confident about the efficacy of this approach to healing.

THE HOMEOPATHIC PARADOX

I was first introduced to the concept of homeopathy more than a decade ago when I decided to attend a workshop on the subject offered by Richard Pitcairn, now widely regarded as the father of veterinary homeopathy in America. As open as I was to new ideas that might enhance my ability to heal my animal patients, what I heard about homeopathy during those introductory sessions was disconcerting, to say the least. The first thing that struck me—and, I might add, shocked me as well—was how the technique flies in the face of generally accepted Western medical practice.

A major idea in homeopathic healing is the use of substances which actually produce the symptoms of the disease the healer wants to cure. These substances are diluted to infinitesimal amounts in solutions before they are given to the patient. Homeopathic theorists teach that the smaller or more diluted the dose, the more powerful the effect.

After receiving a homeopathic medicine, the patient will sometimes experience an intensification of his symptoms before he recovers. This "healing crisis," as it's known, is regarded as part of a process that bolsters the body's internal defense systems against disease. So if you have a fever, a homeopath might give you something that would temporarily increase your fever; or if you have a rash, he might prescribe a minute portion of a plant that produces a similar rash.

Although the use of vaccinations, or small "doses of a disease" to prevent an illness, is somewhat similar to the homeopathic principle, the assumptions of homeopathy run counter to what we are taught in our medical and veterinary schools. There, we are taught that medicines are most effective when used in pharmacologic doses.

Another homeopathic tenet is that a patient should be interviewed in depth in order to identify all the physical and emotional factors that may be contributing to an illness. Western-trained physicians and veterinarians tend to have a much narrower focus: in effect, we put on professional blinders as we try to identify the *specific* cause that underlies the *specific* symptoms. Then we hone in on drugs, surgery, or other procedures that will overcome that single problem—without worrying too much about the broader physical and emotional context from which the patient's condition may have sprung.

Homeopathy gained great popularity in Western nations after being established as an organized system of healing by the German physician Samuel Hahnemann back in the early nineteenth century. In fact, at the beginning of the twentieth century, an estimated one-fourth of all doctors practiced some form of homeopathy. But gradually, the American medical establishment, unable to reconcile homeopathic principles with its own, discouraged the practice. By the 1970s, homeopathy had been generally abandoned by reputable medical people, except in some parts of Europe and India.

In light of these decided differences between homeopathy and what I had been taught in veterinary school, it was understandable that as I heard Pitcairn speak, I found myself wrestling with seemingly contradictory ideas. I wondered if it might actually be possible to reconcile homeopathy with standard Western medicine—even though the two are based on such different views of healing. Since Western-trained physicians and veterinarians generally regard homeopathy as a fringe concept, I was forced to ask myself, "Is there any validity to what I'm thinking? Or am I in the company of a bunch of quacks?"

The answer that came to me was to test homeopathy on

myself before trying it on any of my patients. The focus of my experiment would be a longstanding allergy that had plagued me from childhood. Poison ivy had been the bane of my existence beginning at age twelve, and I had come down with a severe case of it every year since then. I was so sensitive that just passing near the stuff was enough to trigger an outbreak! After I established my practice, I would catch poison ivy just by working on an animal that had brushed up against the plant. My hands and arms would blister and start itching like crazy, and not let up for two weeks. Fourteen straight days of agony.

Over the years, I had tried every treatment in the book—and several folk remedies that weren't in any book—but nothing worked. So I decided to put homeopathy to the acid test and see if it could help me during my next bout with poison ivy. Rhus toxicodendron, the Latin name for the cause of my misery, was available in a homeopathic tablet. I ordered some and waited for a chance to use it.

A few weeks later, I started to get the symptoms, probably as a result of handling a dog that had spent a lot of time outdoors in ivy-infested woods. The itching on my arms had already begun in earnest by the time I placed one of the tablets under my tongue and let it dissolve slowly. As I had been taught, I didn't eat anything just before or after taking the pill.

Fifteen minutes later, the itching stopped. Furthermore, there was no itching for the next twelve hours. After that, the itching started up again, and I took another pill. Once again, within minutes, the itching ceased.

I decided to take the rhus toxicodendron remedy twice a day for the next five days. The itching and the rash stopped spreading and soon began to dry up. Within five days, the poison ivy had disappeared. Over the next few years, controlled by homeopathy, my bouts with poison ivy grew increasingly shorter, and lately I have stopped having any episodes at all.

But I learned quickly that despite my positive results with rhus toxicodendron, I had a long way to go before I could translate my personal experience into an expertise that could be useful to my animal patients.

SUCCESS BEGINS WITH FAILURE

My initial success with homeopathy provided me with a major infusion of confidence. I subsequently learned:

• Double-blind clinical investigations have shown homeopathy to be effective in the treatment of rheumatoid arthritis. In fact, according to a 1980 article in the *British Journal of Clinical Pharmacology,* 82 percent of patients with this condition given a homeopathic medicine improved, in contrast to only 21 percent of those given a placebo.

• Scottish scientists found that giving diluted doses of pollen helped people suffering from hay fever—a result that was reported in October 1986 in the respected British medical journal *The Lancet.*

• In 1989, the *British Medical Journal* reported that homeopathy had been shown to be an effective treatment for fibrositis, a rheumatic disease that is estimated to afflict up to six million people in the United States.

• In a review of 107 controlled clinical trials of homeopathic remedies conducted by three non-homeopathic physicians, eighty-one of the trials demonstrated that homeopathy was effective, according to a report in the *British Medical Journal* in 1991.

Bolstered by such findings, I felt I was ready to venture into homeopathy for my animal patients if the circumstances seemed appropriate. My first opportunity presented itself in the form of a Shetland sheepdog brought to my office by a rough-looking backwoodsman.

"Doc," he said, "I've got this itchy dog here, and I'm wondering if you can help."

The dog was suffering from allergic dermatitis, a condition that a shot of cortisone could relieve. But I sensed that homeopathy might effect a complete cure without the side effects of the drug. So with the owner's consent, I provided a regimen of homeopathic granules for the dog.

About two weeks later, the dog's owner called back and said, "You know, doc, I really like you and your approach, but my dog still itched after taking those little bead-pills you gave him. So I took him to another vet, and he gave him a shot, and the dog was better in twenty-four hours."

Exasperated and somewhat disillusioned, I nevertheless decided to continue with homeopathy, but to choose my patients more judiciously. Not long afterward, a Springer spaniel appeared at my door with his owner, an amateur beekeeper who liked to gather his own honey. The dog had accidentally run into a swarm of bees and had been stung many times. The animal's mouth, eyes, and other parts of his face and body were already horribly swollen. He was obviously in terrible pain, struggling with his breathing and gnawing with his swollen gums as he tried to look up at us through his puffy eyelids.

In a case like this, the conventional medical approach is a shot of cortisone or epinephrine to counter the allergic reaction to the stings, and after my abortive experience with the itchy sheepdog, I was ready to go ahead and give the spaniel an injection. But his owner surprised me by saying, "I hate to say it, but I don't trust traditional medicine. Is there a homeopathic remedy we could try?"

I agreed to go the homeopathic route, with the proviso that if the dog got worse, we would resort to conventional medication. With the dog's labored breathing, I was afraid he might not be far from anaphylactic shock, so I made sure that my epinephrine was close at hand.

The remedy I selected was apis mellifica, a solution derived from the honeybee and its venom, which has been used for many years by homeopaths to treat bee stings, insect bites, jellyfish stings, and similar problems. The solution is prepared by crushing the bee and then diluting one drop of the bee residue with 100 drops of water. This dilution process is then repeated thirty more times until an infinitesimal amount of the bee product is in the solution. No one knows just why homeopathic remedies work this way, although some theorists believe that the tremendous dilution of the solution releases extra energy at the molecular or subatomic level.

Whatever the explanation, this particular remedy worked like a charm. The spaniel took a few granules of the apis mellifica under his tongue, and within minutes started to grow more calm and relaxed. I checked his gums periodically and saw that the swelling was subsiding. Within an hour, there was at least a 50 percent improvement in his condition. By the end of two hours, the swelling had almost completely disappeared and the dog was virtually back to normal.

From that time on, homeopathy became a regular part of my practice. And before long, I had assembled a rather large homeopathic medicine chest with a variety of remarkable remedies that can be used for problems ranging from motion sickness to trauma.

MY HOMEOPATHIC MEDICINE CHEST

An Antidote to Motion Sickness

Cocculus, which comes from powdered seeds of the Indian cockle plant, is one of the major remedies I keep close at hand. Although in large doses this plant can produce vomiting and painful contractions in the arms and legs, in extremely small homeopathic doses there is an opposite set of effects. The most common pet complaint I treat with cocculus is chronic motion sickness, which was the case with a German shepherd from New York City.

The dog's owner wanted me to see her pet to determine whether acupuncture would work for his arthritis, but she faced an even bigger problem transporting the dog to my office in the country. "He vomits every time he steps into the car," she told me. "He shakes, salivates, and turns into a nervous wreck if I just drive around the block. And if I keep him in there longer than a few minutes, he gets violently ill. He's done this

his whole life, since he was just a puppy. We've tried tranquilizers, everything. But nothing works. What can I do?"

I sent her a few granules of homeopathic cocculus in the mail, with instructions to administer five granules an hour before the trip, and although the woman didn't have much confidence in this seemingly obscure remedy, she was willing to try anything. Just before she left, she called me for reassurance: "This is the first time I've ever taken my dog in a car without a heavy tranquilizer. I think *I* need a tranquilizer myself!"

The idea that some little white granules were going to control her dog's nausea and vomiting during a two-hour drive was still too hard to believe, so she equipped herself with extra paper towels, a bottle of spray deodorizer, and other cleaning materials. Then she pulled out onto FDR Drive along the East Side of Manhattan, and hoped.

As mile after mile went by, nothing happened. The German shepherd sat calmly in the backseat, looking out the window. She turned onto the Major Deegan Expressway heading north, and still nothing happened. More than an hour later, as she sped along the interstates leading to my clinic, the dog remained calm and composed, without a hint of distress.

By the time she reached me, the woman was breathless with excitement. "I can't believe it!" she said. "This is the first time in eight years he hasn't been sick in a car."

As this woman discovered, homeopathy can be a powerful tool. Not only can it relieve physical distress, but it can also work to alleviate a host of emotional conditions, including grief.

A Response to Grief

When a pet shows signs of insecurity or agitation arising from abandonment, bereavement, or loneliness, I turn to ignatia, a remedy derived from the St. Ignatius bean. If ingested in large quantities, the St. Ignatius bean can produce hysteria or spasms. Yet somehow, in a paradoxical way that no one can adequately explain, when the bean is vastly diluted in a homeo-

pathic solution, its properties can be translated into an antidote for grief and grief-related emotions.

Some veterinarians would argue that a concept like animal
grief is too anthropomorphic, that such a notion attributes
human characteristics to an animal that just aren't possible or
appropriate. But I'm convinced that animals have emotions
and can miss a loved one just as much as a human being can.
A good example was Suzy, a twelve-year-old cocker spaniel
who was described by her owner as depressed and not eating.
Although the regular veterinarian had run a variety of blood
tests to determine the cause, all the results came back normal.
But it wasn't hard to see that Suzy wasn't normal. She was very
withdrawn, and according to her owner, she lay around all day
on a couch and moped.

"She's wasting away to nothing," the woman lamented.

It turned out that Suzy's physical and emotional decline had
begun about two months before, when she had lost her lit-
termate. The two dogs had been together for twelve years and
were inseparable. Since her sibling's death, Suzy had lost six
pounds—a dangerously large amount for a thirty-pound dog.

"The veterinarian I'd been seeing said the death of the other
dog had nothing to do with Suzy's problems," the woman
told me.

But as far as I could tell, there wasn't any other explanation.
"I think she's grieving," I said, "and there's a remedy that might
help her through this."

I gave her some ignatia tablets to be given to Suzy twice a
day for four days. Precisely four days later, the woman called.
"After the first pill, Suzy's attitude began to change," she reported. "Her energy started picking up and she seemed livelier.
By the second day, she began eating again. Now she's back to
her old self."

How ignatia works to overcome grief is still a mystery. No
one knows whether it triggers some chemical change in the
brain that redresses a systemic imbalance caused by emotional
stress, or whether some other force is at work. But from the
clinical evidence of my practice, I have seen it help not only

dogs like Suzy, but also cats, including a Siamese that was grieving over the loss of her kittens.

The entire litter of four kittens had died right after birth, and the effect on the mother was devastating. The Siamese wandered around the house searching everywhere for her little ones, whining constantly and refusing all efforts of her owner to comfort her. Siamese cats tend to be quite emotional anyway, and this one was close to being incapacitated. Her interest in food began to wane, and it became clear that she would soon die of starvation if we didn't do something to turn her around.

As incredible as it may seem, within twenty-four hours on ignatia the cat began to eat for the first time in several days. Two days later, her agitation and anxiety had evaporated and she was well on the way to a full recovery.

It was apparent to me that ignatia worked well with animals that had lost other animals. But what about animals that had lost beloved *humans?* Would the severing of an interspecies tie be strong enough to trigger a serious depression, which might in turn be relieved by homeopathic healing? The answer came from a German shepherd named King.

The dog's owner was an elegantly dressed woman in her late sixties, who seemed more than a little uncomfortable being in my office. "I'm not sure why I'm here," she explained. "I've already been to two veterinarians, and neither of them was able to find anything wrong with my dog. But to me, he seems very depressed. He has no energy, and he's just not acting like himself."

She explained how King had once been full of joie de vivre. At the drop of a hat, he would jump in the car and enjoy long drives, or run out in the backyard to play. But these days, he wouldn't set foot in the car, and instead of running outside, he just sat on her bed for hours at a time.

"Maybe he's picking it up from me," she said guiltily. "My husband died suddenly a couple of months ago, and I haven't gotten over it. I cry a lot. I suppose King may be depressed because I'm depressed."

Somehow, that explanation seemed a little too pat, and as I probed further I sensed that King wasn't simply mimicking her behavior, he was grieving on his own.

"He was my husband's dog," the woman explained, "and the two of them spent a great deal of time together. Now King often sits near my husband's chair and stares, as though he's expecting him to return."

Shepherds are known to be one-man dogs, intensely loyal and devoted, so it was no surprise to me that King was upset. With a few doses of ignatia, he began to rebound, going for walks with his owner and again running playfully outside. He still liked to lie by his master's chair occasionally, but now there were no whines of lament, only a few sighs of remembrance.

The story didn't end with King. His owner was so delighted by the dog's recovery that she went to a homeopath and started taking ignatia herself. "I don't know if it's all in my head," she told me, "but my depression has lifted. I still miss my husband terribly, but the tremendous weight I was carrying is gone. Now I see hope for me as well as King."

Once I saw how well ignatia worked to assuage grief, I began to use it successfully in related situations that did not involve a death. In one case, a dog was so overcome by loneliness when he was left alone in an apartment during the day that he howled continuously and created havoc by tearing up the carpet. Ignatia calmed him down so much that he no longer carried on, even though he was still all alone while his owner was at work.

Relief from Fear of Loud Noises

When I first heard of a homeopathic remedy for a bad reaction to loud noises, I couldn't quite believe it. How could a solution derived from a plant or mineral cure an animal of its tendency to be excitable? But I soon discovered that this very result could be achieved by using either of two homeopathic treatments: a preparation of the mineral phosphorus; or aconitum napellus, a product of the monkshood plant.

One morning toward the end of summer, I arrived in my office to find a cat who had been quite ill since the Fourth of July after being frightened by firecrackers. As a result of this trauma, she had developed chronic diarrhea and was showing signs of depression. Also, she had developed asthma. Repeated attempts by other veterinarians to treat her with tranquilizers or drugs had failed. Cortisone helped the asthma and bowel problems temporarily, but didn't stop them from recurring. Even a change in the cat's diet hadn't worked.

I prescribed homeopathic phosphorus at a relatively high potency, which in homeopathic terms means an extreme level of dilution. Unlike many other remedies I have used, this one didn't produce an immediate cure. In fact, several weeks passed before we began to see results. But gradually, the diarrhea cleared up, the asthma disappeared completely, and the cat's fear of loud noises was gone.

To many people, and certainly to the medical profession, homeopathy may appear to be closer to sorcery than to science. Because this healing tradition has been outside the medical mainstream for so long, supportive research studies are sparse and seasoned practitioners are few and far between. Certainly, I approached homeopathy with a hefty amount of skepticism when I was first exposed to it. But little by little, over more than a decade, I have become a confirmed believer.

I wish I could claim an understanding of how homeopathy works, but I cannot. Nonetheless, for me the answer is clear. These techniques do facilitate healing, frequently in situations where traditional medical methods fail. So I'll leave it to others to argue. As long as homeopathy helps me accomplish my purpose to heal animals, I'll continue to use it enthusiastically.

PART IV

TEACHINGS

CHAPTER THIRTEEN

Animal Teachings

But ask the beasts, and they will teach you; the birds of the air, and they will tell you . . .

—JOB 12:7

On my journeys along new paths of healing, I have come to expect surprising wonders. But perhaps the greatest wonder of all is that when we enter into a relationship with an animal, we also enter a kind of schoolroom, an atmosphere of learning that can enrich our understanding of life. If we let them, our pets and the wild animals around us can teach us how to experience the fullness of existence in all its exciting complexities. They know secrets that have somehow escaped us, and through them we can plumb eternal truths that can liberate and heal us. One of their most important lessons is the power of compassion.

THE TEACHING OF COMPASSION

By their very presence in our midst, animals awaken in us the desire to respond and to love. Time and again in my practice, animals that need my help have given me the opportunity to be my very best. That's what happened at my clinic late one night when I felt I was too tired to see even one more sick animal. I was about to turn out the light and head for home when an insistent knock came at the door. "Dr. Schoen! Dr. Schoen! It's an emergency!"

I opened the door to find a man drenched from the pouring rain, holding a soggy, limp black cat in his arms. "I found him on the road," the man said. "Probably a stray, hit by a car. Thanks." Before I could even ask another question, he dumped the cat into my arms, got in his car, and drove away.

The cat was unconscious and in shock but still breathing as I rushed him into the examining room. His circulation and capillary refill time were normal. I palpated his abdomen and felt along his body to see if there were any broken bones. Nothing seemed amiss. I began treating him for shock and took x-rays, which showed no internal injuries.

Even in an unconscious state he was a beauty, with a long black shiny coat and white paws that reminded me of Blue, the cat I had owned in college. As I looked at him lying there, the helpless and defenseless victim of human carelessness, my heart stirred with pity. Here was an animal with a concussion whose condition could best be described as a deep retreat from assault, an animal in a state of alarm and trauma. He was not responding to conventional shock therapy and remained comatose. Unless I could jolt the cat back into reaccepting his place in human society, he would die.

What could I do? My adrenaline began to flow until a hidden reserve of strength surged within me. My mind shifted into high gear as I tried to work a miracle.

Arnica montana! That was it. The homeopathic treatment for trauma might be just the thing to turn the cat around. I stopped for a moment, so exhausted I couldn't remember where I had put it. But I did find it and managed to get a few drops of it into the cat. I then watched as he lay there on the table breathing slowly, hoping against hope that he would pull through.

Resting there alone, just the two of us, I sighed deeply and pondered the cat's predicament. Before I realized what I was doing, I heard myself repeating the words I had spoken to Megan when she first turned up at my door with heartworm all those years ago.

"If you make it, I'll keep you," I said aloud.

It took a while. I can't recall how long, but the cat's eyes finally popped open and he lifted his head up and looked around. I continued to wait, gently urging him to trust again in life, and eventually he was walking around my office as though nothing had happened.

All I could do was shake my head in wonder. The cat's life force, or "chi" as the Chinese call it, was so strong that it was instantly clear what I would name him. "Chi," I said. "Let's go home."

That was more than five years ago, and in the ensuing years, this cat has become more than a member of the family—he has taken over the household!

Like Chi, many other animals can inspire something basic in our humanity—some deep need we have to help and to care. In India, that need has been embodied in the form of the bodhisattva Avalokitesvara, who is often depicted with 1000 hands. According to one legend, Avalokitesvara was about to enter Nirvana when he looked back and saw an animal in pain. The sight so touched his heart that he knew he could never be at peace as long as another creature was suffering. When he sought permission from his father to go back and help, his father gave his blessing—and more. He urged him to seek out many others in misery.

"To help you see them," he said, "I'm going to give you a thousand eyes. To help you save them, I'm giving you a thousand hands."

Our animals can show us that we possess extra eyes and hands for compassion, and they may also teach us much more—including some important lessons about the way of forgiveness.

THE TEACHING OF FORGIVENESS

My friend Jackie, who had a penchant for collecting homeless animals, got her latest dog, Van Gogh, at the local pound. He was a pit bull that, despite the breed's sometimes deserved bad reputation, was a white bundle of love, constantly jumping in Jackie's lap and slathering her face with kisses. But when Jackie first saw Van Gogh, she could tell at once that the dog had been abused by a previous owner. The puppy's ears had been cruelly cut off by a teenage boy, who had used ice cubes to numb them before the mutilation. Someone reported the abuse to the authorities. They picked up the boy, sent him home with a slap on the wrist, and put the dog in the pound where Jackie found him.

Van Gogh still had multiple problems. He was hyperactive, and he couldn't go out in the rain because water ran into his ears. He had every reason to be a hostile, vicious dog. But despite the horrible abuse he had suffered, he was not angry and certainly didn't seem to blame Jackie for his condition. He wanted so much to love and be loved that he appeared actually to have forgiven humans—all the humans he has encountered —for their folly. All he wanted to do was pour out on Jackie and anyone else he met his overly generous supply of affection.

This message from a dog about forgiveness when we are the victims of an offense isn't really such a hard lesson to grasp. It is one of the most basic life has to offer. But somehow, with the passions and resentments we harbor, we are inclined to cling to old hurts, hold grudges, and close ourselves off to others for untold wrongs that have been committed against us. But if we remember Van Gogh, perhaps we can begin to move beyond our human restraints to a new kind of freedom. Then, if we are really bold, we can go a step further and learn from our animal friends to be open to personal transformation. Consider what happened to a standoffish calico cat named Daisy when she acquired a more demonstrative roommate.

THE TEACHING OF TRANSFORMATION

Daisy huddled in the back of her cage at the animal shelter, hiding out of sight as Penny began her search for just the right pet. But when Penny heard some squeaky little meows that managed to escape from Daisy across the hall, somehow the sounds seemed to be directed at her. Finally, she found the tiny calico, peering at her tentatively through the bars of her cage—and it was love at first sight.

Penny was so taken with Daisy that she chose to ignore some obvious obstacles that lay in the way. The cat had been caught in the wild, and as far as anyone at the animal shelter could tell, she had never had a real home. From her own background as a psychologist, Penny knew that anyone, animal or human, with that kind of background might be nursing deep emotional wounds that could interfere with the building of normal relationships. But after one look at Daisy, Penny decided she was willing to take a chance.

From the moment Daisy entered Penny's car, it was evident that this wouldn't be an easy experience of animal-human bonding. During that first ride home, Daisy was scared stiff and managed to defecate all over the car seat *and* Penny. Once home, Penny whisked her upstairs to the bathroom, where she got some warm water and started washing the little cat. The animal was too much of a mess to be able to clean herself. As Penny washed one paw and then the next, she talked to Daisy and tried to give her encouragement, all the while assuming that the cat would eventually warm up to her.

But Daisy never allowed herself to get too close, not even after she had been in the house for several months. Sometimes, if she was in a magnanimous mood, she would let Penny pet her. But usually, she would spurn Penny's overtures and scurry away to the far side of the room. Whenever Penny tried to pick her up and cuddle her, it seemed as though Daisy couldn't wait to jump from her arms. She would tense up and wriggle around until she escaped from Penny's embrace onto the floor.

Daisy's standoffish behavior added to Penny's distress in the wake of the recent death of her husband, Leon. One of the things that kept Penny going during this period was Daisy. But she yearned for more affection than the cat seemed able to provide. Since I lived nearby, she often shared with me her desire for a pet that was more responsive. She loved Daisy dearly, she said, but the cat didn't seem to know how to give the kind of love Penny needed.

Then one day a little black cat appeared by my Japanese maple tree. The first day, she ran away. For the next few days, I put a bowl of food out to attract her, and before long I was able to make an approach. And as soon as I got to know her, I realized this was just the cat for Penny. After only a couple of encounters the cat jumped into my arms. Also, she warmed instantly to my touch, purring and purring as soon I petted her.

"This is the cat you've been looking for," I told Penny over the phone.

Penny took her in and called her Lily, but perfect peace and harmony didn't prevail at first. Lily and Daisy had a few false starts at the very beginning, with nasty fights as each cat tried to assert her dominance. But before long they settled in as sisters. Even more significantly, they began to influence each other's behavior. Daisy, the wild sister, showed Lily survival tactics, such as how to go up a tree and how to catch a mouse. Lily never did actually catch a mouse, but following Daisy's example, she did at least try.

In turn, Lily, the warm, affectionate sibling, showed Daisy what it meant to be loving. Lily would give Daisy face baths, licking the calico all over with her tiny tongue. Daisy responded by nuzzling Lily's stomach, in instinctive accord with the maternal love that had been poured out on her.

Soon, Penny was drawn into Lily's love lessons. Daisy would sit on the floor and watch attentively as Lily snuggled up close to Penny on the couch and purred in contentment. One of Lily's favorite pastimes was to lie on Penny's right hand, and if the left hand happened to be dangling nearby, she would give it a gentle lick. Lily also loved to be rubbed on the stomach. She would stretch out on her back and recline in ecstasy as Penny massaged her.

Daisy observed these interactions closely, and before long she was making tentative attempts to follow Lily's example. One day she jumped up on the sofa where Penny was sitting, and to Penny's surprise, she stretched out with her back pressed against Penny's leg. Another time, she actually got on Penny's lap and lingered there, allowing Penny to caress her with long, tender strokes.

Daisy didn't change overnight. But as the weeks stretched into months, the cat that once didn't know how to relate to humans became much more demonstrative and caring. She got so used to sitting in Penny's lap that when Penny took her for drives, Daisy would hop right up onto her lap. The cat became so sensitive to Penny's needs that she actually learned to keep her head low so as not to block Penny's vision as she was driving!

Daisy may never match Lily in the lavishness of her affection, but there was no question that she underwent a remarkable transformation at the feet of her feline teacher. Lily showed an emotionally limited and recalcitrant cat something about expanding her ability to relate and love, and clearly, Daisy took her lessons to heart. And as I contemplate Daisy's surprising changes, I'm reminded that we humans should also be ready to learn as we watch those who are more advanced in loving than we—even if the model we are observing is a pet like Lily the cat.

THE TEACHING OF GRATITUDE

Animals have an inclination toward gratitude that is an intuitive part of their natures. I have seen this sense of appreciation daily in the patients I treat, but also with animals I encounter in my own backyard. A chickadee once flew into a windowpane at my house and bashed his head. I heard the crack against the glass and immediately rushed downstairs to see if the bird was all right.

He was lying on his back on the ground with his eyes closed and his beak open as he breathed fast and hard. I knew he might have a concussion and that the next minute could be his last. So I carefully scooped him up in my hand and rushed inside to get an acupuncture needle and some remedies: arnica for shock and "rescue remedy" for stress.

I gave the bird a drop of these medications through his open beak, and in a matter of seconds he seemed to start breathing more calmly. But his eyes were still closed and his legs were limp, and I was worried that he might be fading. Quickly, I inserted a tiny needle in an acupoint for concussions on the midline on top of the skull and twirled it slowly before removing it. Seconds later, he opened his eyes, shook his head, and breathed a little more steadily.

I was about to give a shout of joy when his eyes closed again and I sensed he was drifting away. I inserted the needle again, and this time his eyes popped open and stayed open. Five minutes later, he started to move his feet, and as I held my index finger under his toes, he grasped it and held on for dear life.

For about fifteen minutes we sat together on the deck overlooking an expanse of farmland. The bird was nestled in the palm of my hand, with his little feet still clutching my finger. His breathing was coming regularly now, and his head kept turning this way and that as he absorbed the details of his new situation. Something wet oozed onto my palm, and I realized that his bodily functions were working just fine.

A few minutes later, he was ready to take his leave. He made a gallant attempt to fly, but he ended up falling flat on my deck. I picked him up and gave him one last treatment with the needle. With that, he took off and flew up to a branch of a spruce tree a few yards away. And then he left.

But a few days later, when I walked out on my deck, I discovered that the chickadee had returned. He was sitting on the bird feeder, and I recognized him because he was the only solitary chickadee to visit. The only other chickadees that frequented the spot always came as a pair. As I acknowledged his presence with a surprised "hello," he flew down to the deck's railing to get a closer look. He didn't seem the least bit afraid. Instead, he looked me straight in the eye and held my gaze for what seemed like a full minute.

I never doubted for a second why he had come back. It was his way of saying "Thank you." Then he cocked his head, gave a little chirp, and flew back up into the spruce tree.

The kindness of a stranger, the generosity of friends, the solicitude of neighbors—all of these call for some sort of acknowledgment or thanks. Although we may forget, animals never do, and with them as our models, we can develop an "attitude of gratitude" that can infuse us with a thankful spirit.

THE TEACHING OF SACRIFICE

When I was teaching a course in Alaska one October, I met a veterinarian by the name of Jim Scott, who was deeply involved in saving eagles and other raptors that had been injured during the massive Exxon *Valdez* oil spill. In the course of his work, he had come across a bald eagle that he called "One Wing" because one of the bird's wings had been destroyed by the spill.

One Wing had been diving for fish in the polluted sea, and oil from the tanker had covered his feathers. For three days he flopped about, trying to keep his balance on the land as rescuers attempted to catch him. The pressure on the wing caused the appendage to snap, and the eagle was finally captured and quieted by one of the rescue teams before he did additional damage to himself.

Unfortunately, it was necessary for Jim to amputate the wing because of the damage that had been done to the fragile bones and tissues. Blood transfusions from other birds, a thorough cleaning, and plenty of attentive care managed to save the bird's life. But of course, One Wing would never fly again, and so he could never be set free.

It's not hard to imagine what it could mean to an eagle, the most royal of all birds, to be unable to fly, unable to soar over the mountains and forests he had once ruled. Many human beings who have lost much less have become thoroughly depressed and given up on life entirely. But One Wing was more resilient. Besides, it would soon be his turn to be a blood donor.

Jim placed the great bird in an aviary in a wildlife rehabilitation center, where other eagles injured during the oil spill were brought for treatment. Like One Wing, many of them also

needed tranfusions, and Jim's one-winged eagle would supply
the lifeblood they required. Without a cry, without resistance,
the bird sat stoically with his one good wing spread out as he
was sedated so that blood could be drawn. The transfusions
would flow into the bodies of his fellow eagles, one after the
other. There was one remarkable period of five days during
which eight eagles received transfusions from One Wing. It was
amazing that his regenerated body could give so much blood.
By all rights, he should have been dead. But One Wing's vital
signs continued to be stable.

Finally, one last eagle was brought in for a transfusion, a
bird that had both wings intact and seemed capable of flying
again if only its lost blood could be replenished. One Wing was
the only one available to act as a donor—but Jim was afraid of
the consequences.

"If I take one more drop of blood from this bird, I'll kill him,"
he said.

He had really come to love One Wing and to respect deeply
his acceptance of self-sacrifice. The eagle almost seemed to
know the possibly dire consequences of giving up so much of
his vital fluids, yet there was no hesitation, no objection. One
Wing's sole purpose in life had become sacrifice for his brother
and sister eagles. If that meant death for him, so be it.

In his own way, Jim said a prayer and thanked One Wing for
the gift of his blood. Then he asked for the eagle's forgiveness
for what he was about to do. His technicians spread One Wing's
good wing out one more time and began to draw the blood.
One Wing's energy ebbed visibly, even as the second eagle
gained strength. When the procedure was finished, the recovering eagle was taken to a different part of the aviary, where it
would eventually be released into the air, ready to resume its
former dominance of the atmosphere.

But One Wing was exhausted, depleted. Nevertheless, after
one final, spontaneous recovery, he survived. And as unlikely
as it may seem, about a year later, another eagle was brought
into his aviary—this one a female that also had only one wing
as a result of the oil spill. After maintaining a proud distance

from each other for months, they one day began a courtship. And before long, out of their union they hatched a beautiful, perfectly formed eaglet.

THE TEACHING OF JOY

I'm at least as aware as the next professional that in the midst of responsibilities and deadlines, life and work can become altogether too serious. That's why I'm so thankful that when I watch them closely and allow them to lead me hither and yon, the animals I'm blessed to meet can add a special kind of joy and playfulness to my life.

I may have received my most powerful lesson about joy when I was visiting the Galápagos Islands in February 1994. This natural wonderland, which lies off the coast of South America and was so eloquently described by Charles Darwin more than a hundred years ago, is the closest thing to heaven for those of us who have devoted our lives to animals. Although I experienced many memorable encounters with untold numbers of species in the Galápagos, the ones that taught me the most about experiencing joy were the sea lions.

One of the first meetings I had with these animals occurred on land, as I was walking toward a spot where they sunned themselves. Suddenly, a big female came storming toward me on the trail and stopped about a foot from where I was standing. The animal must have been six feet long, and I can't even speculate about her weight, but I'm sure she equaled several of me.

My first response was shock: "What do I do now?" I thought. She was barking and I wondered if it was some sort of warning. But as I stood planted there, unable to move, I began to realize that her noises were a greeting more than a challenge. In fact, as I looked at her more closely, I perceived an endearing look in her eyes. Suddenly, I sensed that there was little or no separation between my human self and this massive sea mammal. In some way, we were communing at a very deep level, in a camaraderie that I had never known with such a creature.

Before long, I was surrounded by four baby sea lions. Like their mother, they looked up at me intensely, expressing a special greeting. Two came up to sniff my legs. I felt like asking, "How are you?" But I couldn't. The emotions I felt went far deeper than verbal communication would allow. Then the sea lions drifted away from me and went back about their business of playing and sunning themselves. In the meantime, I knew I had become one of them. I had been invited to participate in their leisure for a time. They were just enjoying life, and they apparently wanted me to feel free to do the same.

That was only the beginning of my interactions with the Galápagos sea lions. They seemed to like to stage reprises of their new relationships, and when I decided to go for a snorkeling expedition in the clear and well-populated waters of the archipelago, they appeared again, as playful as ever. But this time they assumed the role of perhaps the most acrobatic swimmers in the world. Still swimming on the surface, I saw the sea lions spot me from their rocks and then plunge into the water. At that, I dove underwater, and the clearness of the ocean allowed me to see them speeding toward me like mammalian torpedoes.

Before I knew what was happening, I was looking through my goggles directly into a pair of brown sea-lion eyes, only a few inches from my face. Then, like some sort of slippery shadow, he traced the outline of my body, swimming under me, over me, round and round, skirting within inches but never touching. In a flash, he darted away again and began playing and cavorting several feet from me underwater with three or four other sea lions. Periodically, my new friend would look back to see if I was observing him.

It became obvious that I was an integral part of this remarkable underwater celebration. For the sea lions to enjoy themselves completely, it almost seemed that I had to be having fun too. Through their antics and occasional face-to-face "checkups," they indicated their acceptance of me as a creature worthy of being their playmate. Sometimes, a sea lion would even tug at my flipper slightly with his mouth in an apparent effort to get me to move to his rhythms. At other times, the sea lions would take turns tossing me pieces of coral in an underwater game of catch. In some way that I couldn't fully understand, I had become both a spectator and a participant in their games.

After more than an hour of this sea-lion-directed jubilee, I sensed the time was drawing near for me to leave my new friends and head back toward the ship which was carrying us from island to island. But I really didn't want to go. Certainly, I was fatigued, but something compelled me to linger, if only for a few minutes longer. The companionship I was experiencing was unique and exhilarating, too wonderful to let go. With the sea lions, there was no particular agenda, no goal or purpose to the outing—just the opportunity to relax, play, and be joyful.

These sea lions taught me a lesson I'll never forget, and one that I hope I can someday recapture. I learned that you don't have to go out of your way to seek joy. Most likely, joy will find you if you can just free yourself of preconceptions and open your heart to God's creatures. They are more prepared than you realize to draw you into their special fellowship.

CHAPTER FOURTEEN

Megan's Farewell

Do you think dogs will be in heaven? I tell you, they
will be there long before any of us.

—ROBERT LOUIS STEVENSON

I noticed her out of the corner of my eye. Megan was in the backyard, chasing after birds when she tripped ever so slightly. I decided the stumble must have been from a rock or a depression in the grass, because when I looked up from my work, she was running around again as though nothing had happened.

A week later, I caught her limping, almost imperceptibly, on her right front leg. A little bruise, perhaps, or maybe a small scrape from a fall in the woods? An ordinary pet owner might not have thought twice about such a thing. But the minute I saw the limp, I suspected something was wrong. And I could feel myself trembling as the awful conviction started to take hold of me. "She has bone cancer," I thought.

I called out to her, and as she happily bounded over to me, she seemed a robust, perfectly healthy fourteen-year-old golden retriever. But something was telling me otherwise. I immediately opened the door to my jeep and rushed her to my office for a thorough examination.

The x-rays of her leg confirmed what I already feared. As I held the pictures up to the light, I could see the faint beginnings of cancer in her carpus. I looked at Megan, my sweet, gentle friend and teacher, and then back at the pictures in my hand. I started to cry.

The prognosis was terrible. Some veterinarians recommend radiation and chemotherapy, along with amputation to arrest the spread of the disease. But Megan was already getting on in years, and I couldn't put her through such suffering. I wanted to let her go with dignity, with her mind and body intact.

That night I dragged myself home, dreading the task of breaking the news to my wife, Barbara. Megan had been part of our lives since the very beginning of our relationship, and she had even been present at our wedding in our backyard. She had served as a kind of maid of honor, wearing a big pink bow that matched the trim on Barbara's dress, and parking herself between Barbara and me during the ceremony—where she promptly fell asleep!

Megan was lying in front of us by the fireplace as I told Barbara. Together, we cried softly and told Megan how much we loved her. She just lay there looking at us, her eyes knowing, accepting what was to be.

Barbara and I talked about our options and agreed that it was best not to do anything "heroic." Instead, we threw ourselves into the task of making Megan as comfortable as we could. Barbara made her home-cooked organic meals, and I carefully regulated her medication, putting her on natural painkillers and anti-inflammatory agents.

But the truth was that we didn't need to *do* anything for Megan. Just as she had nursed others, she quite naturally started taking care of herself. And as I observed her over the next weeks and months, I realized that through her illness, this dog, who had awakened me to a new way of relating to my patients, was still acting as my teacher. In subtle but important ways, she was still showing me how to *live,* even as she was dying.

I watched amazed as she began to regulate her own activity level. As her cancer progressed, she started slowing down on the walks we took down a nearby country path. Where we used to take one-and-a-half-mile strolls, now after three-quarters of a mile she would stop, sniff some bushes or watch a butterfly, and rest for a while. If Barbara and I kept on walking, Megan wouldn't force herself to plod ahead. She would simply stand on the side of the road sniffing the bushes until we returned, and then walk back home with us. After a few months, she started going half a mile, and then a quarter of a mile, until finally our walks were nothing more than a slow meander up the driveway.

Even more miraculously, as the tumor started getting bigger, Megan sought out a natural spring in back of our house, where she would stick her front leg in the mud and soak it. Instinctively, she had discovered a method of pain relief that has been known for centuries. Mud packs are used in many cultures to heal inflammation, and they are also an old treatment for cancer. No one urged Megan toward this healing method. She just knew.

She also seemed to know that her time was growing short, but she didn't appear to mind at all. Four months had passed since I first detected the tumor, and little by little, she had slowed down to the point where she rarely went out anymore. Around the house, she would hobble a few yards, wagging her tail and sniffing occasionally at a bug or a ball of dust. But mostly she would lie on the floor, drifting off into long naps, while Barbara and I went about our business.

Although Megan seemed untroubled by her condition, I was growing increasingly anxious. I had a three-week lecture series coming up in Norway that had been arranged over a year before. But I didn't want to leave Megan at such a time. I *couldn't* leave her in her final days—for my own peace of mind, as well as for her sake. And even though I knew she was fading rapidly, I couldn't bring myself to put her to sleep just because I was going away.

For weeks, I was in turmoil. My only recourse was to ask Megan. Every day, I would look at her and say, "I don't want to put you to sleep when you're happy and enjoying life. But I can't cancel this lecture. What should I do?" Megan never seemed to give me an answer.

I had tried to postpone the lecture series, but too many people were involved to make that possible. Now, all I could do was make the final preparations for leaving, and hope that Megan would hold out until Barbara and I returned.

As the day of my departure drew closer, I was beside myself. "Megan, I *can't* leave you, you know that!" I would say, looking her in the eyes. She would look back, a deep knowing look, and then wag her tail a little in response.

All the arrangements for Norway were made. A reliable dog-sitter, someone Megan knew, had been lined up; my partner had instructions not to do anything heroic in my absence. Finally, I resigned myself to the fact that I might have to leave Megan without saying a final goodbye. The loving companion that had been with me for so long might have to end her days alone.

But even now, Megan came through to teach me one last lesson. The day before Barbara and I were to leave, we awoke to find Megan breathing heavily, stretched out on the floor at the foot of our bed where she always slept. Her eyes were open, but her body was so leaden that she couldn't lift up her head.

I knelt down with my face next to hers and looked into her eyes. "Megan," I said gently. "This is it, isn't it?"

She had already given her answer. Barbara was crying quietly on the bed as I turned to Megan to acknowledge what was in our hearts. Megan knew. She knew we were leaving, knew we might never see each other again—and so in a final act of love, she was choosing to leave ahead of us.

We sat hugging for a while, all three of us, and then I went downstairs to my office to get the hypodermic needle. When I came back up, Barbara was on the floor with Megan's head resting comfortably in her lap.

For a few moments I sat immobile, staring at Barbara and Megan with the syringe in my hand, not wanting to face the inevitable. Somehow Megan must have heard my thoughts and seen my inner conflict. Because before I could say or do a thing, she lifted her right paw ever so slightly to receive the injection. It was the same paw I had used to save her eleven years before.

That gesture was a summation of her special legacy. As I gently inserted the needle into her vein, I remembered Megan on the day after we first met, when she stretched out her paw to accept the IV that saved her from heartworm. And I remembered her a few years later, when she willingly stretched out that same paw to give her life-saving blood in a transfusion to a wounded dog. In the end, it was clear she died as she had lived—still reaching out to others.

Within seconds it was over. As Barbara cradled her head in her arms, Megan let out a deep sigh and died. We carried her out back and dug a grave, where we buried her and bid our silent farewells.

Yet that goodbye wasn't the end for us. Megan's tremendous impact on my life lives on. I think of her almost daily. Her knowing eyes and loving embrace of others come to mind as I go about my work. Sometimes I become so busy that I fear I'm about to lose my perspective on who I am and what my mission really is. But in those moments of pressure and distraction, the memory of Megan brings me back to true reality—the reality that love is the only force that can make us thoroughly sensitive and responsive to the needs of others, animal and human alike.

Appendix

Veterinary Resources

Send a self-addressed stamped envelope for information on veterinary specialties in your area.

Certified in veterinary acupuncture:

The International Veterinary Acupuncture Society
Box 142, the Mail Station
1750-1 30th Street
Boulder, CO 80301

Certified in veterinary chiropractic care:

American Veterinary Chiropractic Association
P.O. Box 249
Port Byron, IL 61275

Certified in veterinary homeopathy:

Animal Natural Health Center
1283 Lincoln Street
Eugene, OR 97410

Oriented toward holistic animal health care:

American Holistic Veterinary Association
2214 Old Emmorton Road
Bel Air, MD 21015

For further information on nutritional supplements:

Animal Superfoods
P.O. Box 1132
Southwick, MA 01077

Recommended Readings

Animal Massage

Fox, M. *The Healing Touch.* New York, Newmarket Press.
Tellington-Jones, L., and Bruns, U. *An Introduction to the Tellington-Jones Equine Awareness Method.* Millwood, N.Y., Breakthrough Publications, Inc.

Animal Holistic Health Care, Nutrition, and Diets

Frazier, A. *The New Natural Cat.* New York, Penguin Books.
Levy, J. *The Complete Herbal Book for the Dog.* London, Faber & Faber Ltd.
Pitcairn, R. *Natural Health for Dogs and Cats.* Emmaus, Pa., Rodale Press.
Plechner, A., and Zucker, M. *Pet Allergies, Remedies for an Epidemic.* Inglewood, Calif., Very Healthy Enterprises.

Veterinary Homeopathy

Biddis, K. *Homeopathy in Veterinary Practice.* Essex, England, C. W. Daniels Co.
Day, C. *The Homeopathic Treatment of Small Animals.* London, Wigmore Publications Ltd.
Hunter, F. *Homeopathic First-Aid Treatment for Pets.* New York, Thorsons Publishers, Inc.
Macleod, G. *Dogs: Homeopathic Remedies.* Essex, England, C. W. Daniels Co.
Wolf, H. *Your Healthy Cat.* Berkeley, Calif., Homeopathic Educational Services.

References

Chapter Four

Benson, Herbert. *Beyond the Relaxation Response.* New York: Times Books, 1984.

Brown, Raphael, trans. *The Little Flowers of St. Francis.* New York: Image Books, 1958.

Robertson, Arthur. *Language of Effective Listening.* Scott Foresman Professional Books, 1991.

Chapter Eight

Janssens, L. A. A., and De Prins, E. M. "Treatment of thoracolumbar disc disease in dogs by means of acupuncture: A comparison of two techniques." *JAAHA* 25: 169–174, 1989.

Lin, J. H., et al. "Effects of electroacupuncture and gonadotropin-releasing hormone treatments on hormonal changes in anestrous sows." *Am. J. Chin. Med.* 16: 117–126, 1986.

Schoen, A. M. "Introduction to Veterinary Acupuncture." Proceedings, 53rd Annual Meeting, AAHA, 1986.

Chapter Nine

Schoen, A. M. "Acupuncture therapy for chronic Lyme disease in the canine and equine." Proceedings, 17th Annual International Congress on Veterinary Acupuncture, IVAS, 1991.

Chapter Twelve

Fischer, P.; Greenwood, A.; Huskisson, E. C.; et al. "Effect of homeopathic treatment on fibrositis (primary fibromyalgia)." *British Medical Journal* 299: 355–356, 1989.

Gibson, R. G., "Homeopathic therapy in rheumatoid arthritis: Evaluation by double-blind clinical therapeutic trial." *British Journal of Clinical Pharmacology* 9: 453–459, 1980.

Kleijnen, J.; Knipschild, P.; and Riet, G. "Clinical trials of homeopathy." *British Medical Journal* 302: 316–323, 1991.

McSharry, Charles, et al. "Is homeopathy a placebo response? Controlled trial of homeopathic potency, with pollen in hay fever as model." *The Lancet,* October 18, 1986, pp. 881–886.

Acknowledgments

I owe my deepest thanks to a few special individuals for their inspiring commitment to the creation of *Love, Miracles, and Animal Healing*. I wish to thank my literary agents, Herb Katz and Nancy Katz, for approaching me with the concept for this book as well as for their continued superb guidance and invaluable insights through its creation. I am deeply grateful to my collaborator, Pam Proctor, for her creative abilities, writing skills, warmth, and friendship during the writing of this book. I am extremely grateful to my editor at Simon & Schuster, Fred Hills, for his enthusiasm, support, and confidence in the book's message. I also thank Fred's assistant, Laureen Rowland, for her cheerfulness and many efforts on my behalf. I wish to thank my illustrator, Jan MacDougall, for her contribution of sensitive and detailed illustrations. In addition, I wish to express my gratitude to all the other invaluable support staff at Simon & Schuster in the art, marketing, and copyediting departments who have made this book possible. I would like to thank Dr. Martin DeAngelis and Dr. Evan Kanouse for their thorough medical review of the text and Robin Albin for her thoughtful feedback.

I am grateful to my parents for providing such a strong foundation for my personal growth and honoring my desire to march to the beat of a different drummer. I am grateful to my teachers—undergraduate, graduate, and postgraduate, all of whom contributed to my growth as a veterinarian. I am also indebted to my spiritual teachers who supported my personal growth. Finally, I am eternally grateful to my wife, Barbara, for all her love and support throughout our life's journey together.